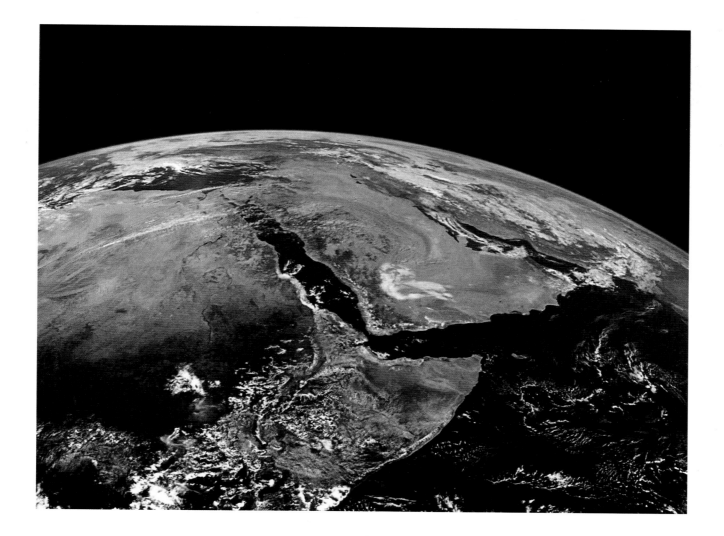

DAVID DOUBILET
ANDREA GHISOTTI
THE
RED SEA

CORAL KINGDOM AT THE DESERT'S EDGE

SMITHMARK

CONTENTS

MY RED SEA *text and photographs by David Doubilet*   *page*   18

THE SECRETS OF THE RED SEA *text by Andrea Ghisotti*   *page*   42

The underwater gardens of the northern Red Sea   *page*   42

Islands and reefs of the central and southern Egypt   *page*   84

Central Red Sea: the fascination of adventure   *page*   96

Southern Red Sea: the last frontier   *page*   131

Texts by
David Doubilet
Andrea Ghisotti

Edited by
Valeria Manferto

Designed by
Patrizia Balocco Lovisetti

Translated by
Antony Shugaar

Text and photographs by David Doubilet have been provided by the agency Grazia Neri - Milano

The publisher would like to thank Dr. Angelo Mojetta for his scientific advice.

© 1994 Edizioni White Star
Via Candido Sassone, 24
13100 Vercelli, Italy

*This edition distributed in U.S.A. and Canada by SMITHMARK Publishers Inc; 16 East 32nd Street , New York, NY 10016
Tel. (212) 532-6600*

SMITHMARK books are available for bulk purchase for sales promotion and premium use. For details write or call the Manager of Special Sales, SMITHMARK Publishers Inc., 16 East 32nd Street, New York, NY 10016; (212)532-6600

This book may be distributed and sold only in the United States of America and Canada. In particular, in no case can it be imported, distributed or sold in Egypt and Israel, and violators will be prosectued to the full extent of the law.

0-8317-7592-0

Printed in Italy by Canale, Torino.

1 At the center of the satellite picture, one can see the long strip of the Red Sea, from the Sinai Peninsula, to the north, extending southward to the Gulf of Aden.
Photograph by NASA.

2-3 Satellite photograph of the Sinai Peninsula, which stands out sharply against the sea waters.
Photograph by NASA.

4-5 A school of glass fish (Parapriacanthus guentheri) emits a burst of shimmering reflected light.
Photograph by Franco Banfi.

6-7 A school of surgeonfish (Naso hexacanthus) swims past the undulating whiplike coral formations.
Photograph by Pierfranco Dilenge.

8-9 Giant gorgonian fans (Gorgonia ventalina) are frequent on the Red Sea.
Photograph by Ariel Fuchs.

10 A blue spotted grouper (Cephalopholis miniata) peers out from among the rocks.
Photograph by Claudio Ziraldo.

11 In the foreground, one can see a crocodile fish (Cociella crocodila), behind a Malabar grouper (Epinephelus malabaricus).
Photograph by V. Paolillo.

12-13 A group of blackspotted grunts (Plectorhynchus gaterinus) seeks protections amongst the crannies of the reef.
Photograph by Vincenzo Paolillo.

14-15 An angelfish (Pomacanthus maculosus) shows off its splendid markings.
Photograph by Pierfranco Dilenge.

16-17 A parrotfish (Scarus sp.) prepares to spend the night by wrapping itself in a blanket of mucus.
Photograph by Kurt Amsler.

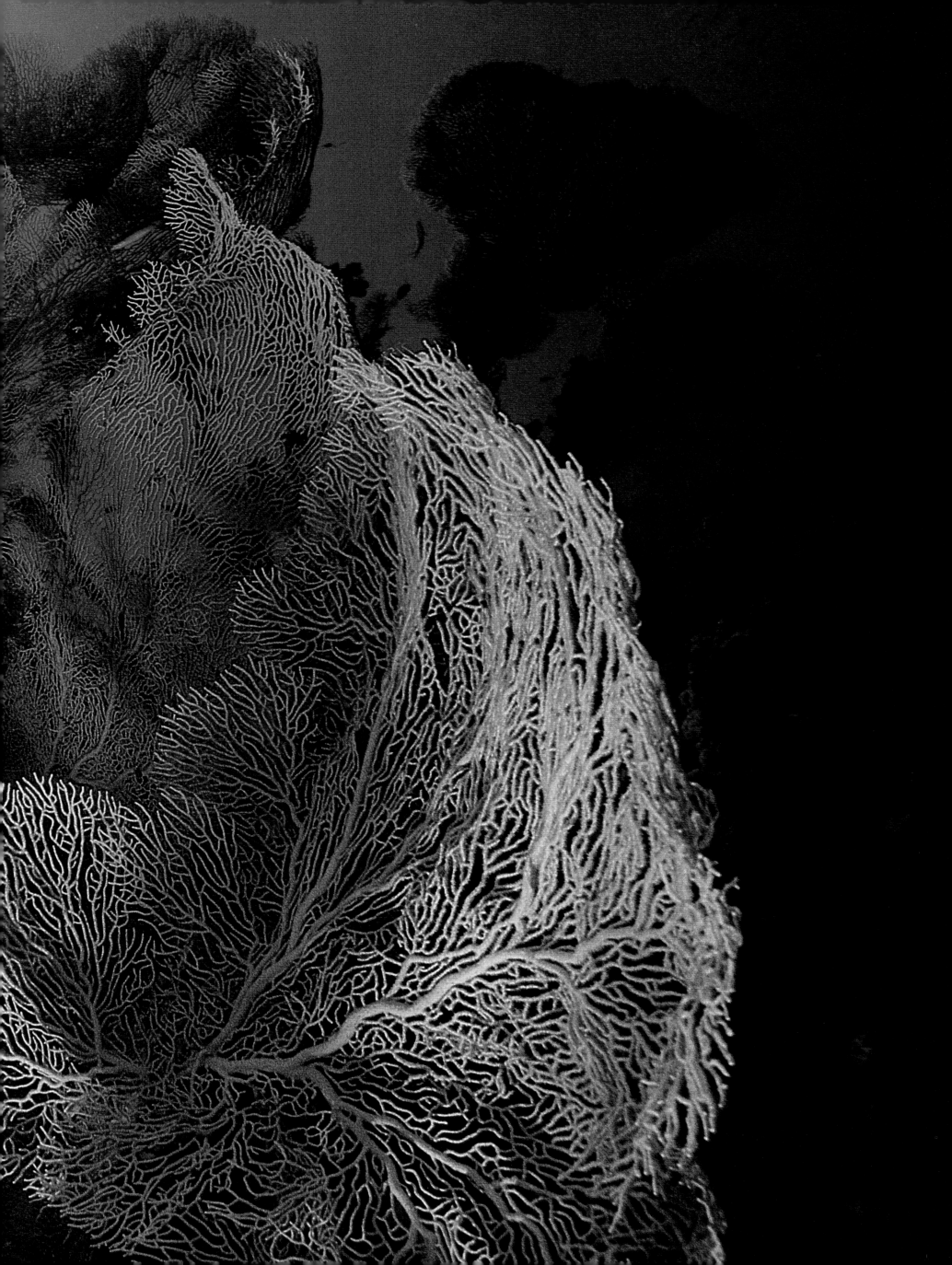

My RED SEA
Text and photographs by David Doubilet

*O*n summer evenings where the sea is flat and the dust from the deserts of Africa and Asia fills the broiling, still air, the Red Sea turns red. The last, long light from the sun is absorbed then reflected until sky and sea blend together and the western horizon seems to pulsate like a heart. The Sinai Mountains turn from yellow to orange then red-purple and finally a dull gray. The smooth surface of the sea is broken by cesio bluefish feeding that make upside down ripples in a pond. Milkfish also feed on plankton. Just under the surface their fin tips stick out of the glassy surface and look like little sharks. Underwater, the sea seems to hold on to the last piece of daylight. The setting sun makes a small dancing palette of light just under the surface and the surrounding sea is strangely an unexpected brighter blue. An underwater afterglow. In this crepuscular hour, the time where the sea changes over from day to night is the time of hunting and hiding, and, as night falls the creatures of the day seek shelter in the reef.

The nocturnal prowlers like the big-eyed red squirrelfish first leave the shadows of the reef.
In the northern part of the Gulf of Aqaba, near Eilat, Israel, the twilight period is very long: the sea becomes a twilight arena.
Undersea naturalist David Fridman and I once watched a group of five lionfish herding a small school of glassy sweepers. The glassy sweepers hung in a ball-shaped school just under the surface. The last afternoon sunlight came through the surface like a spotlight.
It was confusing light for little one inch long glassy sweepers and the lionfish took advantage of it.
They opened their wings and pushed the school into a tighter mass, the pairs of lionfish taking turns, swam through the packed school, striking and swallowing the glassy sweepers.
As the sea gets darker, long-spined sea urchins emerge from their daylight hiding places under the coral. The sea urchins graze on the algae growing on the bottom. The blue triggerfish preys on the urchins. It puffs water through its gills and out its jet engine-like mouth. It sends the urchin tumbling then dives in when the urchin exposes its short bottom spines.
Crinoids or sea lilies also venture out at night.
They climb on spider-like feet to the highest points of the reef and extend their feathery arms to feed in the plankton-filled night sea. Lionfish hover, motionless, above them and as night falls so do the daylight creatures, small fish that confuse the harmless crinoid with the deadly lionfish.
Spanish dancer nudibranches emerge from their daylight hiding places to feed on sponges. The foot long creatures are basically giant sea slugs but their feather-like white gills are open, exposed like flowers to the sea. They have few predators for the poison in the sponges they consume becomes stored in their soft flesh. When disturbed, they undulate through the sea and the Egyptians call them Bedia, named after a famous belly dancer whose liquid movements drove men wild with desire.
On moonless summers nights the sea cucumbers raise off the bottom forming sensuous "S" curves.
They look like begging puppies. In the midnight sea, the "male" sea cucumbers begin to pulsate and then they release clouds of sperm which drift down current to the waiting "females".
By two hours after dark the day's reef creatures are completely hidden, asleep in the endless corridors and alcoves of the reef.
Parrotfish, unicornfish, butterflyfish and groupers hide within the arms of the reef.
Moray eels hunt in the dark arena sliding along the reef, poking their heads into every hole and using their sense of smell and vibration to locate their meals.
The big-eyed squirrelfish also hunt.
Their brilliant red color at night is darker then black, a shadow in the night sea.
The magical dance of the reef continues, therefore, each night, with unchanging rhythms, in the silence of a thousand noises in the ocean deep.

18 The alcyonarians of the Red Sea (Dendronephtya sp.) present an endless array of colors.

19 A school of glass fish (Pempheris vanicolensis) draws back at the approach of scuba divers.

20 A small squid hides amidst the spines of a few sea urchins (Diadema setosum).

20-21 A small number of twobar anemonefish (Amphipirion bicinctus) seem to play amidst the tentacles of a sea anemone.

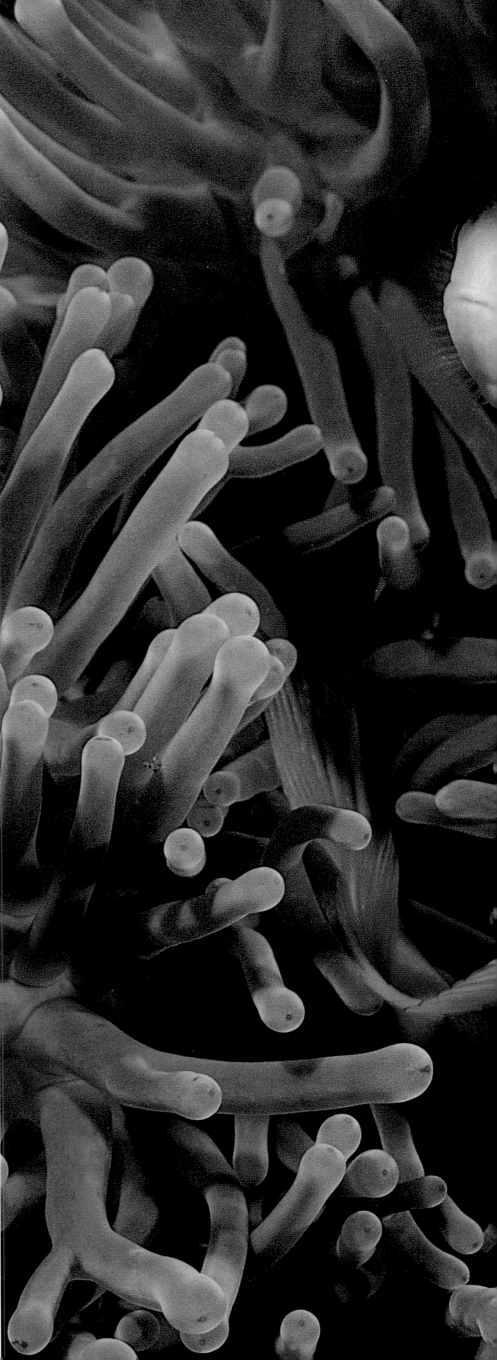

22 A canary blenny
(Ecsemius midas) looks out
cautiously from its grotto.

23 Hidden amidst the coral,
a shortbodied blenny
(Exallia brevis) displays a
cautious attitude.

We left Sharm el-Sheikh at sunset
in our motor vessel, rounded Ras Mohammad and
arrived for the night in the Gulf of Suez.
In the morning we dove on the sunken islands, reefs
actually awash at the very tip of the Ras Mohammad
Peninsula. The reefs have a shallow saddle between
them, but face south toward the open Red Sea. Their
sheer front walls drop into blue-black water and form in
promenades for pelagic creatures, schools of
barracudas, silver jacks, bomber-like dog-tooth tunas
and an occasional shark.
Once there was a funnel cloud of a school of thousands
of Shuri (a species of red snapper), but the fishermen
decimated it.
Ras Mohammad's richness is a product of the strong
currents and water movements that sweep from the
Gulf of Suez to the Gulf of Aqaba.
The deep faces of the sunken islands are covered with
water filled alcyonarian corals - fields of pastel broccoli-
like creatures, their polyps opening and feeding, in the
shade of the cliff coral walls. The vertical reef is veiled
with schools of two inch long orange Anthias.
Millions of them swimming against the current, feeding
on plankton, gliding and finning with the pulsating
current. The entire reef seemed to be rhythmically
breathing with the Red Sea.
Suddenly a patrolling jack swept in and began
attempting to eat Anthias, the reef seemed to flinch,
then the rhythm resumed, feeding, gliding, swimming -
a Red Sea reef that is red and orange draped against a
royal blue sea.
There is no other sea that looks like that, that supports
this kind of living tapestry. As I flew along the reef face
I remembered what Genie Clark once said: "It may be
the richest reef in the world, the most differentiation of
species in the square feet.
The Red Sea has a very thin continental shelf area and
every species must compete for space".
David and I shot along the wall, Asher swam higher,
silhouetted against a midday sun. We paused in an
Anthias coral alcove of the reef and carefully stared at
the endless almost seamless schools of Anthias.
Schools were mostly composed of bright orange
females. Harems of the rare and larger maroon males
with their plume-like dorsal fins stayed in smaller
groups that hung closer to the coral wall.
Swimming among the school were occasional canary
blennies, larger and yellow colored. I saw one attack a
female Anthias.
I chased a canary blenny into its hole. It stuck its
fingertip-sized head out and regarded me with
extraordinary party-colored eyes and twisted two tiny
horns at the top of his head.
I felt a sharp pain in my ear lobe, swiveled around and
found a tiny commando, a yellow three-inch-long sabre
tooth blenny that darted in between the Anthias,
another mimic predator lurking in a herd of tiny orange
cow-like plankton feeders.
The fish had hit me by mistake.

24 A scuba diver looks out over the natural stage of the reef, colored by the infinite hues of alcyonarians.

25 The red Anthias (Anthias squamipinnis) are an inescapable feature of the underwater walls of the coral reef.

*O*n the Gulf of Aqaba side of Ras Mohammad, the coastline opens into a sandy bay called Marsa Bareka. At the tip of Ras Mohammad (the actual headland) there is a place that I called the swimming pool. The reef forms a mini wall which drops down to 40 feet, white sands lap at this coral wall which for some reasons forms a really straight edge, a rare occurrence in the sea. It looks like a swimming pool side and floor and the sand slopes gently down into infinite blue water.

The slope is home to an enormous colony of garden eels that sway back and forth, feeding on plankton, moving with a soundless Near East rhythm.

When you approach the garden eels they disappear as in a dream. The sandy slope is also home to a large colony of thin sand diving fish called Nikkii, a fish named after Genie Clark's son Nikki. When you approach them they also dive into the sand. The sand becomes, in essence, a sea within the sea, a secret blanket that hides the creatures that live in it.

Around a bend in Marsa Bareka is another bend strangely called "The Fishermen's Bend".

On the wall facing the bay there is a coral cave, a little chapel full of silver, glassy sweepers. The cave mouth opens to a sandy sea bed dotted with couch-sized coral patch reefs. A few of these reefs were covered by clouds of glassy sweepers. A group of five yellow and silver jacks fed on the sweepers from above while scorpionfish, red spotted groupers and lionfish lurked in the coral maze below. It was a living food chain that looked like a sculpture.

David and I swam up and sat on the shallow reef table. We watched the blue and white surgeonfish move effortlessly across the reef table slipping in and out of holes like children on a sliding board. The blue striped surgeonfish are found only in the Red Sea and specifically on the top of the reef table in a foot of water. They feed on algae and closely guard their piece of reef, their little algae farm, against other blue and white surgeonfish. As we watched this play of surgeonfish slightly awash on the top of the reef, David put his head up and said: "Look at this. In one view the desert, dry, yellow-brown and the other the sea, bright, blue, full of color."

It was a unique vision in all the world's oceans, alien moonscape tan mountains on top, sliding striped surgeonfish below. The desert sea.

26 top A scorpion fish (Scorpaenopsis diabolicus) lies in ambush, waiting for prey.

26-27 A pair of stone fish (Synanceia verrucosa) camouflage themselves on the rocky sea bed.

27 top Menacing moray eels (Siderea grisea) emerge from their dens, their curiosity aroused.

28-29 These two scorpion fish certainly constitute a dubious pair: in the foreground is a *Scorpaenopsis diabolicus*, and in the background is an *Inimicus filamentosus*.

30-31 This entrancing close-up emphasizes how dangerous the scorpion fish (Scorpaenopsis barbata) can be.

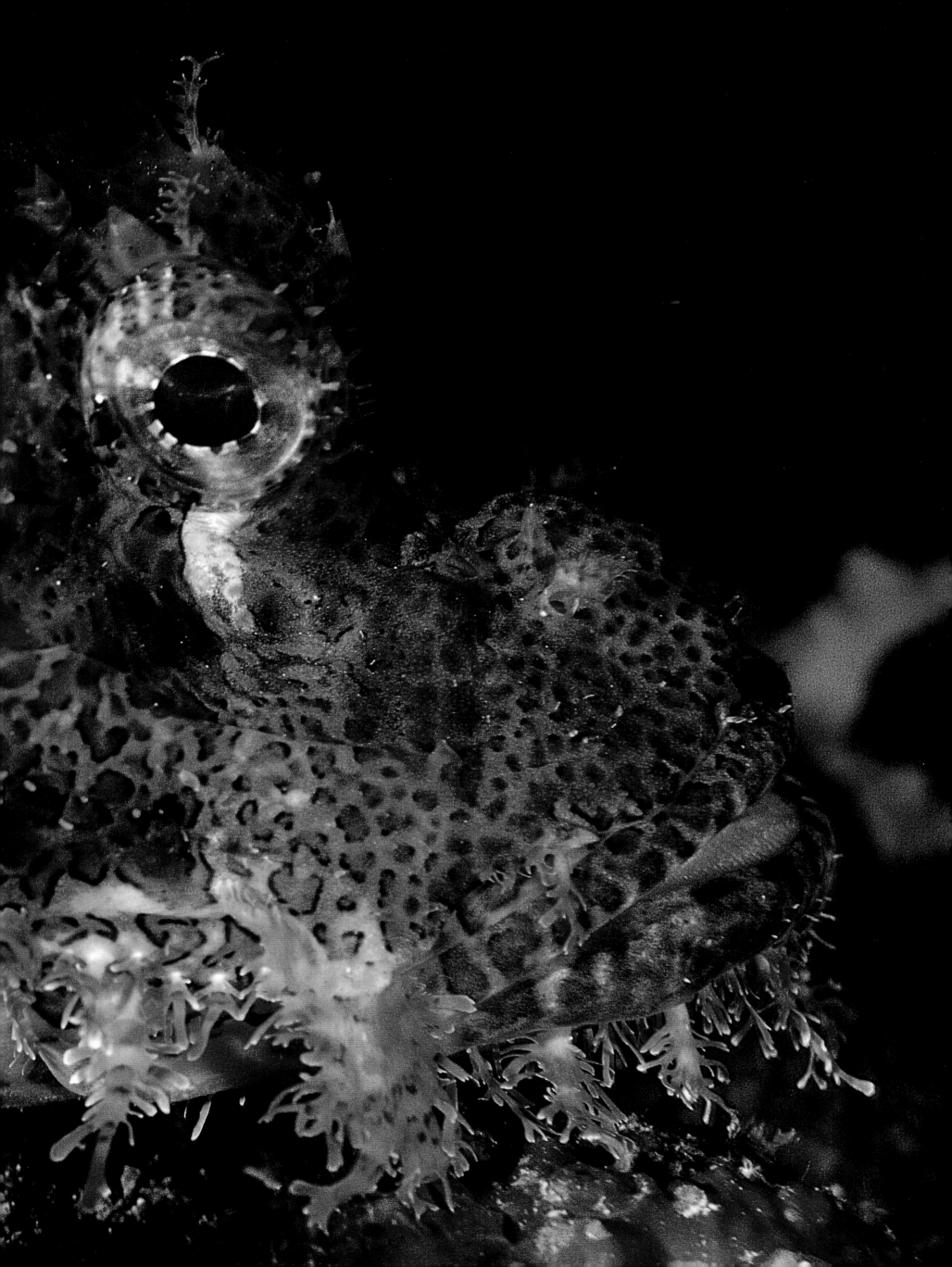

An Egyptian patrol boat came surging around the tip of Ras Mohammad urging our boat to clear the "restricted Fishermen's Bend" area. We returned to Sharm el-Sheikh, picked up four new passengers for a long trip to the south, then the next day cleared out of Sinai on a mirror calm bright afternoon across the Gubal Strait at the opening of the Gulf of Suez. We anchored on the north end of Gubal Island on a reef called Sha'ab Abu Nuhâs.
Iran, squinting at the reef in the afternoon sun said: "This place eats ships, it's usually very rough but you are lucky, it's flat calm, rare".
The reef was like an enormous tooth pointed right up the Gulf of Suez. In rough weather it would be invisible, but in the gleaming afternoon calm, parts of at least five ships stuck out of the water like broken bathtub toys.
In the early evening Asher and I dove on a ship known as the Tile Wreck because it carried a cargo of tile, roofing tile, floor tile, bathroom tile.
The water was clear and I could see at least half the ship. The stern section looked like the bulbous head of a massive whale silhouetted against the evening sea. We swam up the mast and sat on the top which was only a foot below the surface.
The sun had set. The mirror sea was purple in the afterglow and the moon rose as our inflatable boat wound between the tops of the shipwrecks when it came to pick us up.
On the deck of the boat, I looked westward, sea and sky blended together. The afterglow became orange, then red.

32-33 A humphead wrasse (Cheilinus undulatus) swims up to the photographer's lens, with not the slightest sign of fear, showing off the various shades and arabesques of its scales. The humpead wrasses can attain remarkable sizes, at times growing to be 6.5 feet in length, or even larger.

34 The naturalist David Fridman chases after a yellowspotted burrfish (Chilomycterus spilostylus) which has taken up its distinctive defensive position out of fear.

34-35 Frightened by the closeness of the scuba divers, two yellowspotted burrfish have blown themselves up, thus extending the intimidating spines that are arrayed in seventeen rows.

A *light morning wind pushed*
small wavelets across the top of Sha'ab Abu Nuhâs.
The reef sloped down to a sandy bottom at 110 feet,
and the 300-feet-long hulk of the P & O mailsteamer
Carnatic nestled at the foot of the reef. It actually looked
like another reef, for the steel hull was pimpled by
thousands of hard coral growths. We swam above the
graceful curves of Carnatic's clipper-style bow, that,
in September 1869, sank in the dangerous water of
Sha'ab Abu Nuhâs.
In a mild current we swam the length of the ship.
Carnatic was, for her day, a creation of the absolute
highest technology, a supersonic Concorde, an iron
ship with a steam power-plant, turning the propellor,
and changing the lives of people all over the world.
But its hull shape still followed the time-tested curves
of a wind-powered clipper ship.
We paused by the graceful overhanging stern, then
ascended the slope of the deadly Abu Nuhâs Reef.
In the afternoon, our boat pulled anchor and headed
south. A north wind began to blow, out of a mild, blue,
clear sky with a thin white border at the horizon.
The Red Sea marched south with us, in endless,
uneven lines of whitecaps. The following sea pushed
under the stern and she began her elephant dance, a
stately wiggle followed by a hissing surf down the
front part of the wave.
I took to my cabin which was the master stateroom -
polished teak and thick carpets - a posh cave. "Posh",
I ruminated, "is a Red Sea word", born in the days
when the Red Sea was a blue highway, a passage to
India. Wise, rich passengers coming out from England
on the sister ships of the ill-fated Carnatic, would
carefully book a room on the port side, which faced
eastward. The deadly sun emerging from the night
across the Saudi Arabian Peninsula would not really
get hot until mid-morning. Then the air would begin to
broil, and the iron ship, thumping south, in a following
sea and wind, would be trapped in a bubble of oven-
hot still air. As the sun reached its zenith, then clattered
downward across the western sky, the super-heated air
would make the starboard cabins unbearable,
especially, in the days of stiff upper lips and stiff British
woolen collars. The starboard side cabins facing the
sunset (the hottest time of the day in the desert) would
be roasting. The port side cabins would be in the
shade. For the passage home to England, the process
would be reversed, port side out, starboard side home.
The word "posh" entered the English language.
In the early evening, the Brothers, Al Akhwan, popped
out of an empty sea, like brown, sandstone
mushrooms. The north Brother had a tall, striped light-
house, manned by the Egyptian Lighthouse Service.
In the yellow evening light, two keepers wandered
down to watch our passage around a maelstrom of
white water northern reefs. The only safe anchorage
was the southern Little Brother. Iran put the anchor on
the dead part of the table coral, and the boat drifted
backwards like a dinghy tethered to a yacht.
In the morning we went diving on the top of a wedding

cake of a reef. The brown sandstone Little Brother
spiraled down into the depths, tier after tier.
The Little Brother island was a pinnacle, the spire of a
mountain that drifted ledge upon ledge downward in
the very blue, very clear water. Seas from the rising
north wind wrapped around the island, and there was
a very little calm lee. Densely packed schools of orange
Anthias rose and fell with the current that coursed
along the reef face.

36 A small goby
(Bryaninops natans),
distinguished by its violet eye
and the partial transparency
of its body, rests upon an
acropora corals.

37 A longnose hawkfish
(Oxycirrhites typus)
camouflages itself amidst
the branches of a gorgonian.

38-39 A dense group of
anthias (Anthias
squamipinnis) bob and sway
in front of a pink gorgonian.

40-41 In an aerial view, the
peninsula of Ras
Mohammad, the far southern
point of the Sinai, extends
out into the open sea.

THE SECRETS OF THE RED SEA

Text by Andrea Ghisotti

THE UNDERWATER GARDENS
OF THE NORTHERN RED SEA

*I*t's here, it's here, hurry, come on! It is Renzo who calls us excitedly. I grab my Nikonos and I dive into the water, swimming toward the point where Renzo emerged. At first hazy, and then increasingly clear in its unmistakable outlines, we see the outline of an old ship resting on the coral bed of white sand. What a strange shape... it seems like a sailing ship, say a clipper, with a narrow, squared-off poop deck, and a huge tiller, but then I realize that I am wrong, that is a propellor, a huge three-bladed screw partly dug down into the sand. Like ghosts, the empty shafts rise upward that once held dangling lifeboats, witnesses to a drama that has been played out a thousand times in the waters of the entire planet. I make my way into the area beneath the poop deck, wedging my way through the supports of the deck boards - the work of the water and the passage of time have worked to disintegrate those boards, and now it is possible to see the ship in a sort of cross-section. Enormous schools of silvery fish stream around me on either side as I pass through and giving the scene a perfect touch of theatricality that a stage of this sort seems to demand. Fierce turkeyfish, proudly float at the center of the stage with self-sufficient calm. Moving past the old first-class and second-class staterooms, now little more than empty spaces that give directly onto the sections of the bilge, I reach the central portion of the ship, where the old boiler stands in its awful majesty, the heart of the motor apparatus, with a few relics of the single smokestack and a welter of contorted tubes. This is where the hull split and sheared, the sign of a structural collapse that must have occurred quite a few years ago, to judge from the quantity of accretion that has accumulated on the sheet metal. On the sand of the sea floor, extended like fingers reaching out into the water, two huge metal masts and a welter of lines, now sheathed in a colorful coating of mother-of-pearl. Now I understand, sails and engine on the same ship mean that what I here behold are the remains of one of those magnificent vessels that stood midway between the golden period of sailing ships and the final triumph of steam ships, when ship-owners and captains appreciated the mechanical reliability of steam but did not yet feel courageous enough to abandon entirely the absolute certainty of wind propulsion. What a marvelous find, a rare example of those few years that transformed and revolutionized the history of maritime transport! Here is the crow's-nest, where terrified eyes may have spotted the reef roiling and foaming under the bow, just before the fatal impact.

42-43 A twobar anemonefish
(Amphiprion bicinctus)
emerges from its safe refuge
amidst the tentacles of a sea
anemone.
Photograph
by Alberto Muro Pelliconi.

44 top Huge coral
concretions have developed
along the entire hull of a
tugboat, overcome by the
insidious waters of the Red Sea.
Photograph by Andrea Ghisotti.

44 center The stern of the
Carnatic, which sank on the
reef of Sha'ab Abu Nuhâs in
1869, lies on the sea bed 80
feet under the water.
Photograph by Itamar Grinberg.

44 bottom The huge bow of
a transport ship juts
dramatically out into the vast
space of the underwater world.
Photograph by Claudio Ziraldo.

45 The silhouette of the cargo
ship *Ghiannis D.* stands out
sharply against the dangerous
reef of Sha'ab Abu Nuhas, 82
feet under the water.
Photograph
by Frederic Di Meglio.

*I am swept by a series of indescribable feelings, I realize
that I am one of the first human beings to discover the
remains of this great shipwreck, to read and reconstruct
the pages of a tragedy by observing that which the sea
has hidden and preserved for so many years. This is one
of the reasons that has pushed me to explore the seas of
the globe, and which in these few instants attains the
highest and most acute levels of intensity. Toward the
bow, there are some holds, where my fellow divers are
pawing through the wreckage in search of more of the
legendary old green-glass oval bottles, badly molded,
some of which had the names of Indian cities impressed
upon them: Bombay, Calcutta, or else Soda Water. All
around there are shattered cases of wood, which have
released dozens of wine bottles onto the sea floor, each
marked with an enormous N.2. As we dig into the
muddy floor, we also find a big wooden block for the
raising and lowering of the sails, and a little parasol
with the canvas still perfectly preserved. Lastly, we
come upon the bow, one of the most handsome pieces
of work that I have ever seen underwater, long and
tapered like that of the Rhone in the Virgin Islands,
another relic from that period, likewise driven by sail
and by steam. These bows are truly amazing structures,
long and slender like those of clipper ships, narrow and
sharp so that they slice through the waves like a knife.
Of the bowsprit, however, there is not a trace, but we can
see very clearly the huge metal ring that once held it into
place. In the evening, after an exciting trip across the
strait of Gubal, we offer up a toast to the success of the
expedition, uncorking one of the bottles of N.2 salvaged
from the hold of the wreckage. The cork crumbles into
dust and an unspeakable stench wafts out of the bottle,
like an evil spirit in some fairy tale, poisoning the air. The
quest for the name of this mysterious hulk was no less
adventuresome than the discovery of the wreck itself.
We had very little information upon which to work: a
period that ranged between the middle and the end of
the nineteenth century, a fragment of porcelain from a
plate with an illegible scrap of a name, and the probable
English home port, given the bottles of wine and soda
water. A true needle in the haystack, as I was to realize
just a little later while poring over the endless stack of
pages of the registers of Lloyd's, which featured the
names of hundreds of ships that had gone down in the
Red Sea. I was beginning to realize just how many prows
had cloven those waves ever since antiquity. In effect,
ever since the days of the ancient Egyptians, this had
been the true route along which to reach the Indies, and
along this route passed ships bearing the merchandise
that was then conveyed in vehicles of all sorts
throughout Europe: spices above all, but also precious
stones, pearls, fabrics, ivory, ebony, cinnamon, incense,
myrrh, tortoise shells, rhinoceros horns, elephants, and
slaves. At first, one could not reach India by sea, but
only Aden, the ancient Eudaimon, in Arabia, where
goods of all sorts were trans-shipped by the Arab and
Indian sailors, who alone knew - and kept jealously
secret - the schedules and behavior of the monsoon
winds of the Indian Ocean.*

The dominion of Arabs and Indians over these waters was loosened for the first time when king Solomon made an agreement with the finest sailors of his time, the Phoenicians of Tyre, allowing them to build a fleet on the beaches of the Red Sea which they then sailed to India. Nor did these daring sailors stop at this admittedly very risky undertaking. It now seems to be clearly demonstrated that the Phoenicians did what not even Herodotus wanted to credit - that is, they circumnavigated Africa, sailing down along the Red Sea, reaching out to the Cape of Good Hope, and then sailing north along Africa's western coast, regaining the Mediterranean along Gibraltar, an undertaking that required about two years. Aside from these remarkable exploits, however, the Red Sea remained the route linking

the known world with the East and with Africa, the entryway to markets and merchandise that were radically different from those of the Mediterranean and Europe. And this is precisely why, ever since antiquity, sailors and traders felt the need to establish an easier route connecting the Mediterranean to the rest of the world, without forcing them to fall back upon interminable camel caravans stretching from Clysma (now Suez) to Alexandria, or else along other caravan roads, along the eastern coast of the Red Sea. Probably as far back as the times of Ramses II, around 1300 B.C., construction was undertaken for a canal, known as the Canal of the Pharaohs, which was ideally meant to connect the eastern arm of the Nile with the Bitter Lakes, a project that was broken off a number of times due to insurmountable obstacles and the gradually filling up of the canal with wind-blown sand. Work was started again almost as many times, until the Roman emperor Trajan turned his hand and forces to it in A.D. 106, and apparently succeeded in the construction of the Amnis Traianus, a navigable canal that created a link between the Red Sea and the Mediterranean, and which

seems to have survived intact for some seven centuries following his death, right up until the decline of the Byzantine Empire. Despite the fact that it was possible to sail this route directly now, it would seem that not many ships did so, and it seems that special fleets were stationed in the Red Sea for this purpose, shuttling back and forth to the east. The chief harbor for the ownership and departure of these fleets, from the earliest times, seems to have been the port of Berenice, set in a natural inlet that was rather well sheltered from the prevailing winds. But let no one believe that Berenice was a particularly large port. For most of the year, it was a sort of semi-abandoned outpost, without a supply of fresh water (the water was transported from Kalalat, some five miles away). When a fleet or a ship set out for Aden, then the port sprang to life, with merchants, sailors, and adventurers who were trying their luck in the sea trades. The ships were laden with everything that could be sold or bartered in eastern markets: clothing, blankets, tunics, copper, glass objects, swords, spears, cooking pots, and recipients of all sorts. The ships would set sail with the unfailing north wind, and sailing down the Red Sea presented no particular problems, aside from the numerous coral reefs which were menaces to be avoided, by sailing far from the shores, in the central channel of the Red Sea, the channel used even today by large ships. The destination port was, for many centuries, Eudaimon, which had over time become a crucial trading center, where western and eastern merchants came together until, in the first century B.C., Hippalos succeeded in spiriting away from the Arabs and Indians the secrets of the monsoon seasons - all one had to do was to set out in the right months, and crossing the Indian Ocean became a simple task. This discovery opened the way to the Indies for the Romans, who had been hindered on the land route by clashes with the Parthians. In the space of just a few years, trade with the east grew enormously, to the point that Pliny wrote in 77 B.C. that each year the east absorbed goods from the west to a value of not less than fifty million sestertii, and that the goods that were in turn exported from there and sold on European markets were then sold at a hundred times their original cost. The departure from Berenice took place around the beginning of August, and the return was scheduled toward January, with ships laden with merchandise more precious than that of the Arabs: diamonds, sapphires, turquoise, lapis lazuli, agates, cornelian, pearls, silk, cotton, and the increasingly sought-after spices, indispensable in the refined cuisine of the Roman patricians. Such wealth could hardly fail to stimulate the greed of a number of coast-dwelling peoples along the Sinai Peninsula and the Gulf of Aqaba, who at first did no more than to strip those ships that ran aground on the reefs, but who then went on to outfit full-fledged pirate ships, which would attack the defenseless cargo ships in the open sea, until losses became excessive, prompting a massive Roman response. The port of Myos Hormos was set up to the north of Berenice, as an anti-pirate base, from which the lethal quadriremes would set out on missions

52 top   A parrotfish
(Cetoscarus bicolor), a typical
inhabitant of the reef, hides
amidst the branches of a
madrepore.
Photograph
by Pierfranco Dilenge.

52-53 This extreme close-up emphasizes the powerful beak with which the parrotfish (Scarus ferrugineus) feeds, ripping out large pieces of coral. Photograph by Jones-Shimlock/Secret Sea.

53 top The name of parrotfish comes from the bright colorings and the powerful beak, a product of the fusion of the front teeth. In this picture, we can see a *Scarus ferrugineus.* Photograph by Itamar Grinberg.

of destruction, sacking and burning the pirate coves and "punishing them as they deserved..." (Diodorus). If the descent along the Red Sea no longer presented major problems, sailing back up was far less of a task, with north winds that hindered the navigation for ten months out of the year, conceding a slight truce only in the fall. This problem was often insoluble, and it led to a number of different solutions. At times, merchants chose to land their goods in southern ports along the Arabian coast, transferring the goods onto small craft that could easily sail north while hugging the coast, taking advantage of local breezes and sheltering in the lee of the coast when the north winds blew too savagely. The Romans preferred, instead, to land on the western coasts, and to send the goods northward in long caravans, toward the Nile, where they were moved onward in river vessels all the way up to Alexandria. Nor was the problem entirely solved in later centuries. As late as the nineteenth century, when Lieutenant Waghorn developed the extremely efficient postal service between the United Kingdom and India, the English often had trouble reaching Suez in their great merchantmen. And that is why the newly developed steamships were immediately put into service along this route, not so much for their relatively unassuming speed, when compared with the incredible fleetness of clippers of the time, but because with a steamship it was possible to be sure of travelling successfully up the Red Sea against the wind, in a way that had been previously unthinkable. Beginning in the middle of the nineteenth century, there was a considerable stream of this sort of ship in the waters of the Red Sea, a traffic which was chiefly controlled by the English, who did everything within their power to hinder the construction of the Suez Canal, fearing that it would deprive them of their exclusive control of maritime traffic with the Far East. In 1846, the Société d'études du Canal de Suez *was set up, and England did all she could to keep this company from receiving the railroad rights of way it had requested in 1849 for the construction of tracks from Alexandria to Cairo and Suez. A full-fledged trade war, in which however England was ultimately unsuccessful; work began on the canal, and the waterway was finally inaugurated on 17 November 1869, amidst grandiose celebrations, culminating in a performance of* Aida, *which the sovereign Ismail had commissioned from Giuseppe Verdi.*

All of this information was surfacing as I continued to rummage through the archives in an effort to give a name to my ship, with a fragment of plate with an undecipherable scrawl, limited to a specific number of years by inescapable logic, but still too broad a period to be able to choose a name amongst the many ships that went down during these years. From the archives of the Jerusalem Post, *I had learned of a ship called the* Dunraven, *a wreck that was quite similar to the one I had seen, and which had gone down in the same general area, on the opposite shore of the Strait of Gobal, a deadly stretch of sea which here draws into a funnel, generating tumultuous currents that have caused countless shipwrecks throughout history, as is indicated by the impressive hulks of powerful modern ships which lie helpless on the reef, ground down and reduced to sad hulks by the terrifying force of the sea. In the hold of the* Dunraven, *the same bottles of Soda Water had been found as were in our wreck, and this ship as well, which went down in 1876, had been a mixed sail-and-steam vessel. There were a great many similarities, therefore, and the long list of possible wrecks began to narrow down noticeably. Another useful item of information emerged from the decipherment of the legend on the fragment of plate found in the hold:* Real Ironstone China, *a type of ceramics very much like porcelain, made principally by the Longport company, which shut down in 1876 however. I had learned that in the holds of our ship, human bones had been found, and this cleared the list of all the ships that had gone down without loss of life. A ham radio operator helped me to stay in contact with Renzo, who was working as an instructor and guide on board a charter boat, operating in the area, and as soon as he was free from his duties, he would dive down to our wreck. It was to be another name that would finally solve the mystery, and the ring of the phone rocked me out of my bed at dawn. It was Renzo in a state of high excitement: "Andrea," he cried, "I know that the name begins with the letters CA." "Carnatic," I shouted back, "Carnatic, there is only one ship on the list that starts with the letters CA - Carnatic!" It had been a shipwreck that had been much discussed at the time, and which had shaken English public sentiment. It was just two months prior to the inauguration of the Suez Canal, and the steam-and-sail driven vessel* Carnatic *had set sail for Bombay and Calcutta, with a cargo of all sorts of merchandise, the inevitable sacks of mail for the extremely efficient English postal service, and 230 passengers. It appeared to be an uneventful journey, with a calm sea, but at one in the morning on 13 September 1869, breakers were sighted off the bow. P.B. Jones, the captain immediately ordered "helm hard a-port" and "all steam abaft" but the reef of Sha'ab Abu Nuhâs drew inexorably closer, and then the hull ground onto it. There was a bit of panic on board, mitigated by the proverbial English self-control, and damages did not seem particularly serious. A delegation of passengers told the captain that they intended to remain on board until the steamer* Sumatra,

another ship operated by the same company, the
Peninsular & Oriental Steam Navigation Co., could
arrive to continue them on their way. On the morning
of the 14th, the ship suddenly split in half, settling to
the bottom, and dragging with it the twenty-seven
persons who died in the wreck. During our dives into
the wreck of this once-and-now-famous ship, the
frequent destination of charter cruises, visited each
year by hundreds of scuba divers, we discovered the
remains of three other more modern ships in the same
stretch of seabed, a clear demonstration of just how
dangerous these waters can be. Very few areas in the
world are more rife with adventures for those in search
of wrecks than the waters of the northern Red Sea.
Recently, the Thistlegorm, an armed cargo ship full of
wartime materiel, was found; it had been destined to
the English troops on the Egyptian front during the
Second World War, and was bombed and sunk by
German fighters before it could cross through the Suez
Canal, after circumnavigating Africa.
Cousteau was the first to find it in 1951-1952, and he
shot unforgettable scenes for his film, The World of
Silence, which can certainly be considered one of the
landmarks of underwater documentaries. In the various
scenes, one sees the divers in the team, wearing the
very quaint triple-tanks scuba gear of the time and the
double hose regulator Mistral.
The divers wear only bathing suits, and wander
around on the bridge, the decks, and in the holds of the
ship, discovering the ship's bell, which was to give up
the magical name of the vessel, once it was cleared of
incrustations.

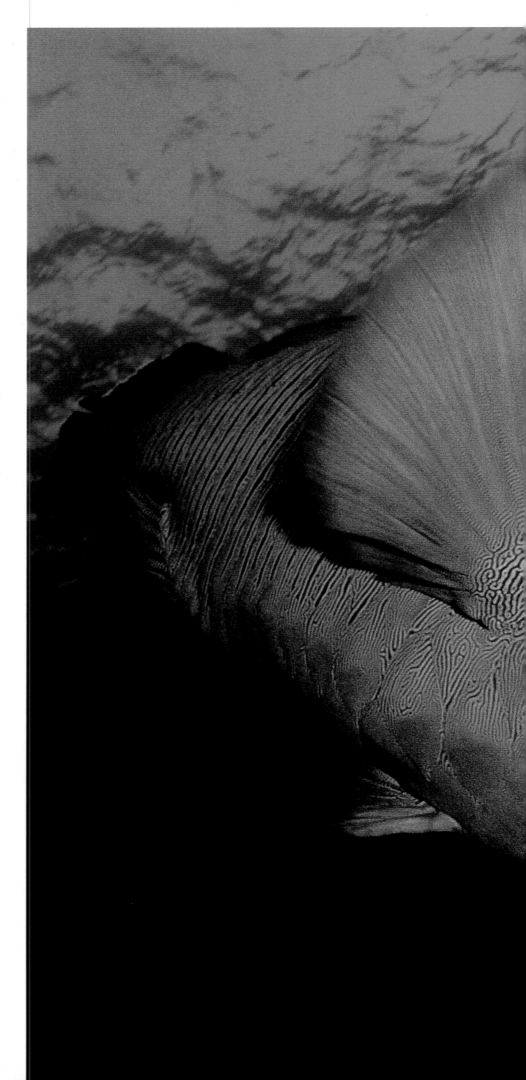

56-57 A large humphead
wrasse (Cheilinus
undulatus)
steers sharply in front of the
photographer's lens.
Photograph by Lionel Pozzoli.

57 top   Titan triggerfish
(Balistoides viridiscens) are
distinguished by extremely
powerful teeth that allow the
fish to feed on crustaceans
and sea urchins; in particular,
the latter are the foundation
of the triggerfish's diet.
Photograph by Urs Moeckli.

58-59 A sharksucker (Echeneis naucrates) remains firmly fastened to the body of a humphead wrasse (Cheilinus undulatus) by means of a powerful suction cup attached to the center of its head
Photograph by Andrea Ghisotti.

60-61 The picture shows the glittering life of the underwater reef. In the foreground, surrounded by the inevitable glass fish (Parapriacanthus guentheri), a delicate fan of gorgonians opens up.
Photograph by Franco Banfi.

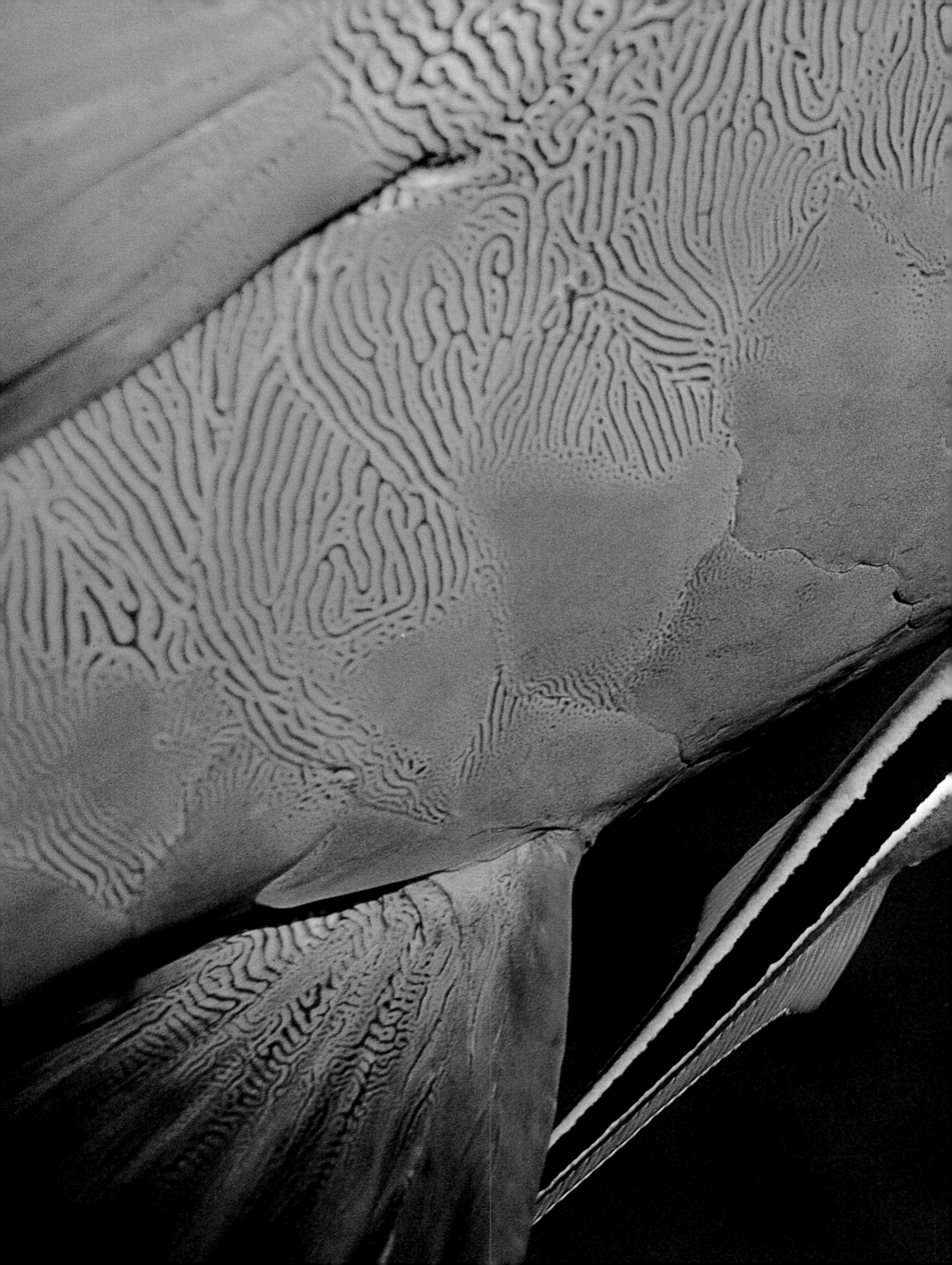

62 A small starfish (Fromia sp.) almost seems to be imprisoned amidst the open polyps of a coral. Photograph by Jeff Rotman.

63 An *Acropora* with a pale rose hue gives haven to a starfish that alternates a bright red color with small purple dots. Photograph by Itamar Grinberg.

64-65 Two tiny blennies (Helcogramma sp.) sleep on a branch of alcyonarians (Dendronephthya sp.), camouflaging themselves amidst the colorful background. Photograph by Jeff Rotman.

66-67 A school of surgeonfish (Naso hexacanthus) swim close to the reef; in the foreground, one can see the inevitable, undulating alcyonarians. Photograph by Carl Roessler.

68-69 Along the coasts, the water glitters with the remarkable colors typical of the reef.
Photograph by Andrea Ghisotti.

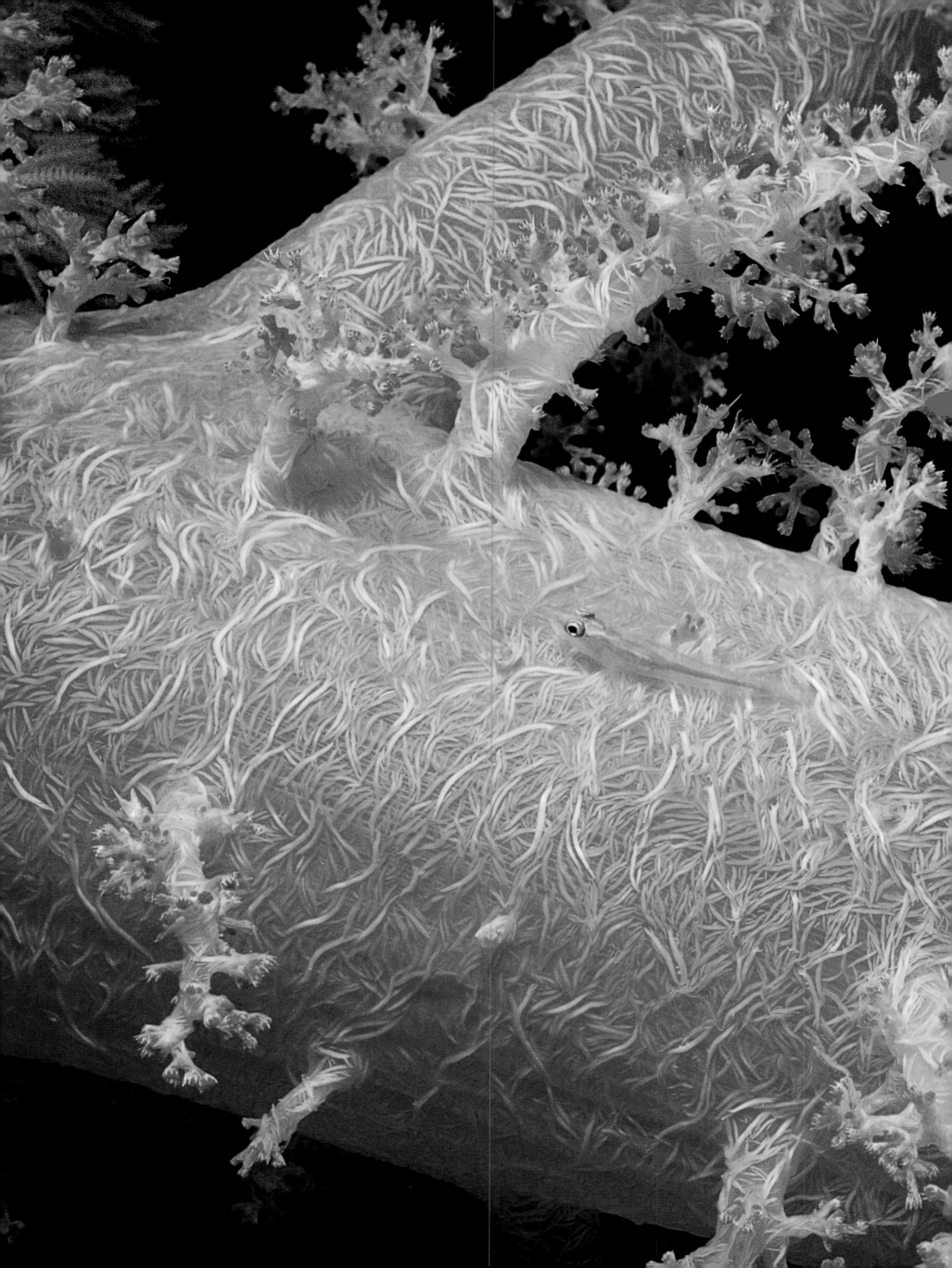

These waters are truly crowded with shipwrecks, but it would be an error to suppose that the scuba divers who come here from all over the world do so primarily or exclusively to explore this underwater cemetery. The northern Red Sea is, first and foremost, one of the finest underwater gardens in the world, and a number of the dives that can be made here have a place all their own in the list of the top ten dives in the seas of the world. An ideal underwater itinerary can begin at Eilat, in Israel, with a special dive... on dry land, where, instead of the classical somersault down into the deep, one descends the steps that lead to an underwater observatory, connected by a catwalk to the municipal aquarium of this seaside city. The structure is built on a sandy bottom where a number of small colored madrepores grow, inhabited by a lavish fauna. Anyone, therefore, whether a scuba diver or not, whether a child or an elderly person, can thus enjoy the beauty of a tropical sea bed, admiring it directly through the big plate-glass windows of this unusual observatory, gaining a sense of the excitement of the sea that has pushed more than one visitor to begin diving or learning how.
The dives in this stretch of sea are certainly interesting, especially during the night, when the glittering and multicolored fish that can be observed during the day, take refuge in the madrepores for the evening's rest, while other animals, ranging from the graceful crinoids to the hastily hurrying hermit-crabs, become the commanders of the field.
Ras Mohammad, the extreme tip of the Sinai, deserves a chapter all its own, and it has every right to be considered one of the finest dives in the world. All of the capes and the points that extend toward the open sea in general represent points of extreme interest for scuba divers, chiefly because of the powerful streams and currents that bring nourishment to a lively population. Ras Mohammad is not only a cape, but it is the final watershed between the Gulf of Aqaba and the Gulf of Suez, the two northern branches of the Red Sea. Above the surface of the water is a rocky promontory set as a buffer for the winds, surrounded by desert wastes that rise toward the interior in remarkable landscapes, with mountain chains that, a short distance from the sea, reach remarkable heights, all the way to the summit of Mount Sinai, which gradually accumulates a snow peak as the winter sets on.

70 top From the windows of the Underwater Observatory of Eilat, it is possible for anyone to take a look into the wonders of the underwater world.
Photograph
by Cesare Gerolimetto.

70-71 The Observatory of Eilat also possesses a small submarine, the *Jacqueline*, in which tourists can visit the surrounding seabeds. In the background, it is possible to see the futuristic structure of the Observatory.
Photograph by Itamar Grinberg.

71 top left The *Jacqueline* can reach a depth of 131 feet.
Photograph by Itamar Grinberg.

71 top right At Eilat, a splendid dolphinarium has been created, the Dolphin Reef, which extends over 100,000 square feet and contains dolphins, as well as rays, sea turtles, moray eels, and numerous other fish typical of the coral sea beds.
Photograph by Itamar Grinberg.

Underwater, the contrast with the nearby desert becomes even sharper and more strident. The water is almost always crystal clear and the coral seabeds are an unforgettable explosion of life and color. The alcyonarians, in particular, are abundant and brightly colored, so much so that one would begin to think that the adjective of Red that is applied to this sea should be attributed to the remarkable concentration of these coelenterates. Just off shore from the point, two coral towers rise up from a considerable depth, with steep walls that plunge downward toward the open sea where barracudas and snappers are so plentiful that a scuba diver is rapidly lost amidst huge living walls of fish. There was a time when these waters were densely populated by sharks, which could even be observed in safety by a coastal shelf that acquired the name of Shark Observatory. Today, only the occasional small Carcharhinidae or a minute barrier shark makes an occasional appearance, immediately returning to deeper waters, far from the coming and going of boats and ships. Ras Mohammad has correctly been declared a natural park, and as such it is protected and regulated. Somewhat less than delighted with this development are the moray eels and the humphead wrasses which had become accustomed to eating the hard-boiled eggs brought to them by scuba divers. The scene was always strange and amusing. The humphead wrasses, large and well-fed, with their distinctive shock shaped like a tuft of hair above their forehead, immediately detected the scent of the eggs, and they would cluster around impatiently, their large bovine eyes carefully scrutinizing every move and gesture. If the scuba diver was slow or a little careless, he would suddenly find his hand lodged securely inside the vacuum-cleaner-like mouth of the big fish, which would gently remove the egg alone and then, as if nothing at all had happened, went back to staring at the diver with an innocent air, so that divers often wondered for an instant if the egg had truly been stolen in so amazing a fashion. And then, when the diver's reason seemed permanently unhinged, the fish would spit out the cracked egg shell. Today, it is forbidden to feed these fish, which had become addicted to the food brought by the divers, losing their natural ability to procure food for themselves.

72-73 The cape of Ras Mohammad, the extreme southern tip of the Sinai, is without a doubt the most famous location for diving in the Red Sea.
Photograph by Itamar Grinberg.

74-75 This aerial view shows us the four reefs that stand before the strait of Tiran - in the foreground is the Gordon Reef, followed by the Thomas Reef, the Woodhouse Reef, and the Jackson Reef.
Photograph by Itamar Grinberg.

76 top   The Naama Bay,
near Sharm el-Sheikh, has
become in recent years one
of the most heavily visited
tourist attractions in the Sinai.
Photograph by Itamar Grinberg.

76 bottom Twilight captures
the little marina of Sharm el-
Shekh. Once a tiny fishing
village, Sharm el-Sheikh's
advantageous location up-
to-date tourist attraction.
Potograph
by Marcello Bertinetti

77 A school of jacks
(Carangoides bajad) swims
through the clear water,
glittering with silvery
reflections.
Photograph by Jeff Rotman.

How can I describe Ras Mohammad in just a few lines
of prose? Its gorgonians, which look out over the steep
north slope of the eastern tower, are giant and splendid
fans which extend into the open sea, creating a sort of
natural barrier, which serves as a fitting backdrop to
the close-travelling groups of snappers. Continuing our
tour in a clockwise direction, the wall drops sheer to a
level of 230 to 330 feet, and still further down, with
cliffs and canyons sinking down to depths of almost
2600 feet. Down at this depth, there are probably still
tiger sharks and hammerhead sharks, which may
swim up in the night to poke around the shallows, the
same areas which provide the most excitement to scuba
divers and photographers during the daytime.
The wealth of fish is absolutely amazing, especially
between the two towers, where an area extends that is
from 26 to 33 feet deep, with a sandy bottom alternating
with madrepores, which may be the richest and liveliest
area in the entire region. In just one hour of diving one
can see more species of fish than in an entire week in
the rest of the Red Sea. Toward land is Anemone City,
one of the largest colonies of sea anemones, with their
accompanying twobar anemonefish that I have ever
seen on a dive, a genuine underwater Mexico City.
A number of other dives in the area are high level, though
perhaps less complete than Ras Mohammad. Such is
the case with the reefs of the strait of Tiran, unfailingly
adorned with the carcasses of sunken ships, like every
other zone in this area. These zones, too, are swept by
powerful currents, and as such are densely populated
with those creatures that require plankton to live and
grow, such as alcyonarians and gorgonians, which in
certain points attain remarkable sizes and numbers.
The entire stretch of sea around Sharm el-Sheikh, now
under Egyptian sovereignty, in underwater terms, was
discovered by the Israelis following the Six-Day War,
and equipped its natural beauty with appropriate
structures. Already in the Seventies, these areas were
well known among European divers, Swiss and
German foremost among them, but at the time there
was that and little more, nothing like the boom of the
last five or six years, which is transforming Sharm el-
Sheikh into the leading tourist attraction in the Egyptian
Red Sea, a status that was once reserved to Hurghada.
Anyone who traveled to these areas just ten years ago
is left breathless.
Naama Bay, the long and slightly savage beach that
stood just four miles to the north of Sharm, with a hotel
or two and a few jury-rigged structures, and where one
could freely set up a tent on the beach, is now an
elegant beachfront, shaded by palm trees, lined with
an unbroken row of luxurious hotels, entire avenues of
boutiques and gift shops, discotheques, charming little
restaurants, diving centers, and nautical and marine
activities, just like in the best known resorts of the rest
of the world. The slightly adventurous charm of years
gone by has been lost once and for all, and a great
many of us miss the vacations there organized on the
run, with a camper or an old pickup truck parked by
the side of the road, on the edge of that unbelievable

78 and 79 top   Glass fish
(Parapriacanthus guentheri)
form compact schools which
move around, driven by the
current.
Photographs by Jeff Rotman.

79 bottom Elegant lion fish
(Pterois volitans) hover under
the surface of the water.
Photograph by Kurt Amsler.

80-81 In this picture, one
sees the spines of the
Acanthaster planci, a starfish
that lives on coral.
Photograph by Jeff Rotman.

82-83 The coral polips
agitates their tentacles in the
dark waters of the night.
Photograph
by Itamar Grinberg.

water that made one forget and forgive all the heat and discomfort suffered out of the water. The seafloor, happily, has not been subjected to the damage one might fear, though a few dives, such as that to the Temple, are no longer as fine as they were in our recollections. Hurghada, on the other hand, on the far side of the strait of Gubal, has enjoyed a more gradual development of tourism. In Italy, it became famous at the time of the expeditions of Ludovico Mares, a pioneering scuba diver and the founder of the company that manufactures diving equipment and that bears his name; in the Sixties he organized a series of expeditions in great style, inviting the leading names in diving at the time. The goal, openly declared in those years, so uninformed about ecology, was to test on large prey,

the new airguns and explosive projectile heads, better known among Italians as lupara, *the word used to describe the shotgun. The underwater rifle which was developed during these expeditions was finally given the name of the location, so that the* Vicojet *with an extended airtank was called the* Vicojet Hurghada. *The sea in those years was pure and uncontaminated, and everything had yet to be discovered. A boat took us out to Shadwan, the barren island that offered mute testimony to so many shipwrecks, and we would go hunting for sharks, jacks, and barracudas. Today Hurghada is a Miami Beach of the Red Sea coast, linked by daily flights to the principal cities of Europe. Almost thirty years of scuba-diving tourists have not done much to harm the coral formations, which are even now among the most spectacular in the world. Perhaps they are a bit too perfect, genuine, perfectly manicured English gardens for scuba divers, abounding with alcyonarians and swarming with reef fish, with the same chromatic richness and the same lack of rude wildlife as a botanical garden, nothing like the raw charm of the southern Red Sea. Therefore, one should not expect to have any noteworthy encounters, as the sharks are small and timid. And yet excitement is there to be had, and we can offer the experiences of a friend of ours, Alessandro Carletti, as an example. Carletti dove into an unspoiled and very deep shallow water together with Adriano Bicciato, who runs a diving center here in Hurghada. This was a day with a great deal of current, one of those days in which one has the certainty that the sea is different, bubbly and jumpy. The top of the shallow water was about 115 feet under the surface, a plunge straight down through the deep blue water, so as to prevent being dragged off elsewhere, onto prohibitive sea beds. While the two of them were dropping into the deep, huge schools of jacks would zip around them in all directions, with a decidedly different dynamic from the calm and peaceful form of swimming that the scuba divers were used to seeing. Before they touched down on the bed of the shallow water, there suddenly appeared a compact little squadron of hammerhead sharks about eight feet in length, and with a smartly executed about-face, these sharks moved into line on the heels of my friends, tailing them insistently. In the meanwhile, a number of* Carcharhinidae *rose up from the deep, the usual grey reef sharks, and they too were strangely excited that day. Alessandro and Adriano understood that they were for some reason in the wrong place at the wrong time, and they began to ascend, followed from a diminishing distance by the hammerhead sharks. And so a fairly harrowing ascent began, with the sharks increasingly excited and frenzied, a wall of water above them to be moved through at a deliberate pace, and the current dragging them out toward the open sea, and the boat nowhere in sight. Finally, they heard the reassuring tum-tum of the diesel engine, which drove off the sharks, and was followed by a jump into the decompression chamber with all their equipment still on, and a big sigh of relief.*

ISLANDS AND REEFS OF THE CENTRAL AND SOUTHERN EGYPT

*I*f we leave the diving centers, restaurants, discotheques, boutiques, and comfortable hotels of the north, where scuba diving is by now just as easy and tame as in all the heavily touristed areas, then one sees the doors of adventure opening toward the great south, the true Red Sea, which even today, as close as one may be to Europe, and as long as one may have been coming as a visitor, remains one of the fascinating and unpredictable seas in the world, a reliable source of excitement and unforgettable adventures for those who are not too dependent upon air conditioning and the austere tranquility of the leading hotels. The only way to visit this long channel (which runs for hundreds and hundreds of miles toward the south, wedged in between Africa and Asia

and lapping at the coasts of Egypt, Sudan, Eritrea, and Djibouti, on the one side, and Israel, Jordan, Saudi Arabia, and Yemen on the other) is by boat. Charter boats in most cases, or else by private boat for those few fortunate individuals who have plenty of time to spare. Embarking at Hurghada or at Sharm el-Sheikh, one explores the northern reefs, with numerous wrecks lying here and there, a fairly undemanding cruise which requires a week or two, and which allows a diver to sniff the air of adventure of the open Red Sea, even though the cruises are always within sight of land and short in duration.

Things are different if one begins to head south. After a sail which may be quite rocky, due to the rough waters, one sights the Brothers Islands, two small volcanic islets which break the surface of the Red Sea some hundred miles from the Sinai coast. The larger of the two islands, Big Brother, is about 1300 feet long and a lighthouse was built on it by the English in 1880, and is still manned by Egyptian troops. Landing is forbidden, but a friendly chat with the troops garrisoned there may help to open a few doors and one may very well be allowed to climb up to the top of the lighthouse, whence one can enjoy the brilliant panorama of the mottled blue

nuances of the coastal reefs. Little Brother, the smaller island, is little more than a reef a few dozen feet across, and it lies about 2500 feet away from the larger island. Diving down into the steep sea beds of the two islands, one sees things that one will remember for the rest of one's life. The almost incessant north wind creates a problematical situation in terms of currents, and even the most experienced divers may find themselves in a difficult situation. The underwater walls that plunge down to sea beds almost 1000 feet below the surface, and the considerable distance from the coasts, are - in turn - a reliable assurance of exciting adventures. As is always the case underwater, one may make special dives or things may be fairly ordinary, but in any case well above average. Sharks make themselves quite at home here. When diving by day, one is likely to meet up with hammerhead sharks and grey sharks which emerge from the depths to examine newcomers with curiosity. At night, on the other hand, it is best to stay away from these waters. Off the Brothers Islands, too, there is a handsome wreck: it is the Aida II, which went down in 1957. The Aida was a military craft, which provided transportation for the troops manning the lighthouse, and which hit the reef of the big island in September of 1957, sinking in a sailing position, with the prow some 100 feet under the surface, and the stern some 230 feet under. The hull is heavily overgrown with huge gorgonians and alcyonarians, and the remarkable visibility makes it possible to take spectacular photographs. If one decides to head further south, in the heart of the Red Sea one comes across Dedalus Reef, which may be considered the handsomest spot for diving in all of Egypt, and certainly one of the most outstanding in the Red Sea as a whole. Rising up from the deepest of abysses, this solitary reef, where extremely few divers have made descents, considering the danger and time involved in reaching the location, and considering that there are no safe anchorages whatever.

Underwater, however, one soon forgets about the fears and discomforts of the voyage, and falls under the spell of this lavish reef - both incredibly intact and just swarming with fish. One could run into any underwater creature imaginable, from manta rays to walls of jacks, sharks, sea turtles, dolphins, and huge tuna. This site is located some sixty miles to the north of Ras Banas, the cape that concludes the gulf of the ancient port of Berenice, a leading commercial terminus in antiquity. Quite recently, it became possible to venture as far as this along the coast road, passing numerous military check points, until Ras Quland, a long dock in considerable disrepair, where mineral products are shipped. Here, during the summer months, there is a charter boat which will take divers as far as the islet of Zabargad, on the border with Sudan. Today, these routes are forgotten and out of the way, but there was a time when they teemed with merchantmen and caravans. Egyptians, Phoenicians, and Romans plied these waters with trade fleets that would nowadays strike the sailors dumb with amazement, in comparison

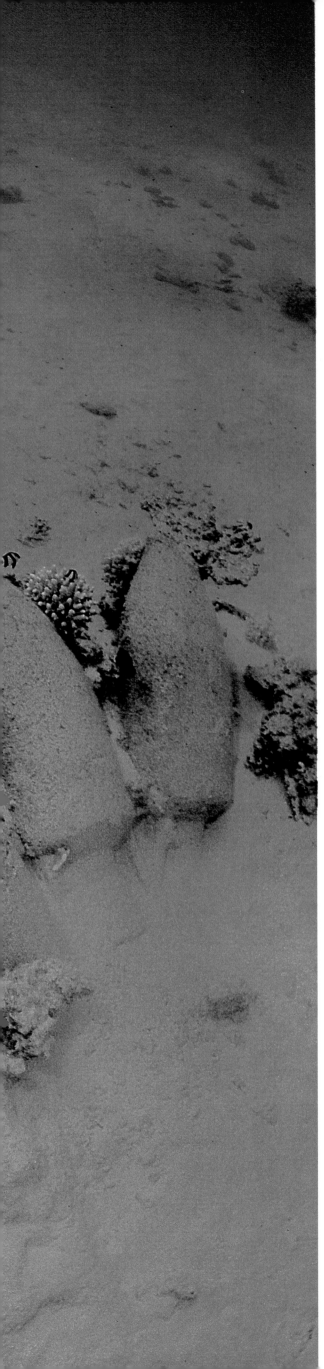

86-87 Near the island of Zabargad, on Dolphin Reef, dozens of Roman amphorae have been found, part of the cargo of one of the many merchant vessels that plied the Red Sea.
Photograph
by Pierfranco Dilenge.

with the tiny sailboats that navigate here nowadays, coasting and doing a little fishing. One should hardly be amazed at the discovery of dozens of Roman amphorae on Dolphin Reef, one of the numerous reefs that make up the enormous ridge of Fury Shoal. To judge by the distinctive shape of the amphorae, this was quite likely a wreck that occurred under the Empire, and was caused by the Roman cargo ship driving into the reef. Given the position, to the north of Ras Banas, and therefore north of Berenice, one might suppose that the ship was sailing toward the northern ports of the Red Sea, probably toward Myos Hormos or Clysma, and perhaps to sail through the legendary Amnis Traianus, all the way to the Mediterranean. Zabargad was already well known in Roman times, and its mines were worked for a number of centuries. It seems well established now that it was nothing other than the ancient Topazos, whose mines yielded the finest gold-ore-bearing rock in the world ever since the times of the pharaohs of the XVIII dynasty (around 1500 B.C.). The Greeks gave the name of Topazion to the remarkably beautiful gem of an olive green color (hence the modern name of olivine), clear and transparent. Today, with the name of topaz, we are indicating an entirely different stone, but at the time this term indicated all precious stones ranging in color from green to yellow.

Zabargad is of considerable geological interest, and has been studied at length during various expeditions during the Seventies and Eighties; in particular, we would like to mention the expedition carried out by the GRSTS, Gruppo Ricerche Scientifiche e Subacquee (Scientific and Underwater Research Group) of Florence, which completed a naturalistic and geological expedition in which Italian, Egyptian, and French scientists participated.

Zabargad appears to be a "tectonic" island, which has surfaced due to the pressure of the Arab plate drifting into the African plate. And as this happened, minerals were brought to the surface from the earth's mantle which had never been altered by a volcanic environment. Therefore, this is one of the very few places, if not the only place on the planet, where it is possible to study the geological, chemical, and physical makeup of the minerals that from the earth's mantle, or at least that part of it which normally lies about 12 miles beneath our feet. In the island, it is possible to observe three peridotitic masses, the largest of which is called Peridot Hill, and which stands 770 feet in height. And it is on this highland that the mines and quarries were dug for the extraction of olivine.

Today, the island is completely abandoned, and a tour of the place imparts all of the melancholy charm of those places that have experienced a more prosperous and active past. The only possible landing site is that in front of the small eastern lowland, where an old stone dock has been built, and where the final remains of two sheds and a few rusting metallic structures survive. The old, roofless shacks are today home to a number of fish hawks, or ospreys, which make their nests among the old rocks.

87 top The distinctive reddish higlights of Zabargad, the ancient Topazos, contrast with the deep blue of the sea. This fabled quarried the precious green gems of "olivine" from its mines.
Photograph by Vincenzo Paolillo

87 bottom A long wooden walkway offers access to the lighthouse that looms above Dedalus Reef, one of the most enchanting locations for diving in the Egyptian Red Sea.
Photograph by Vincenzo Paolillo.

88-89 A large eagle ray (Dasyatis sp.) as it lies resting on the sandy bottom.
Photograph by Itamar Grinberg.

90-91 A whale shark (Rhincodon typus) swims along, followed by a crowd of sharksucker (Echeneis naucrates).
Photograph by Kevin Deacon.

A stroll in the heat of the burning sun leads to the base of Peridot Hill, where it is possible to find the rusting rotting hulks of abandoned mining carts and huge piles of shattered rocks, amidst which it is fairly easy to find little chunks of rather cloudy olivine. Further up, along the mountain slopes, there are mine shafts, dug out of the rock by men wielding picks.

The best way to get an idea of the horrible working conditions that prevailed years ago, when unhappy wretches would break their backs working away in these mines, is simply to climb inside. As soon as you make your way past the entrance, your throat is clamped shut by a suffocating and oppressive heat. The tunnels are exceedingly narrow, and it is often necessary to crawl along or even to wriggle on your stomach, while the ceiling is not at all shored up, and it is easy to imagine how many accidents must have been caused by suddenly tunnel collapses.

And yet from 1500 B.C. until the last war, Zabargad was a working mining operation, where splendid olivine was extracted, some of which now form part of the crown treasure of Russia. One should not suppose that these are gems of particular monetary worth, although their value fluctuates according to the laws of supply and demand, with a slight leap upward when the mines of this island were closed. Olivine is found in other locations, it is true, but it would seem that olivine from Zabargad is the most perfect and transparent in the world.

From the island's highlands, it is possible to enjoy an incredible view of the lagoons that surround it in every direction. The southern coast, in particular, offers some truly dreamlike views, with an endless succession of shades and nuances of turquoise, green, and blue, which contrast amiably with the powerful yellow of the sun-scorched coast. A dive along the edge of the southern lagoon is an unforgettable experience.

Wearing a diving mask and fins, one can explore the labyrinth of madrepores, worming one's way into the series of clefts and corridors that open directly onto the external underwater wall of the reef. This wall drops sheer and vertical for several dozens of feet, and one can look out over the precipice as if one were on a balcony, admiring the delirious riot of colors of alcyonarians and gorgonians waving over the abyss; the abyss in turn yields up an unending progression of schools of jacks, barracuda, snappers, and sharks. Another fantastic spot for diving is right in front of the only small dock on the island.

Here the madrepores have gone wild in crevices with narrow walls that join together further up, creating an unusual architecture that is quite evocative, especially when one dives at night. During the expedition of the Gruppo Ricerche Scientifiche e Tecniche Subacquee (GRSTS)*, Olschky, Notarbartolo, Cinelli, and Solaini were impressed by the exceptional concentration of fish, foremost among them sharks, around the islet of Rock Island, which lies just a little over three miles away from Zabargad in a southeasterly direction. I personally did not notice any greater numbers than what I have found elsewhere, although this is clearly one of the finest areas in the Red Sea.*

Rocky Island has sheer walls rising straight up over the sea, and it is difficult to get past the ten to thirteen feet of sheer drop that separates the small beaches from the highlands of the central island.

The climb is worth the effort, however, as the entire highland is covered with thousands upon thousands of terns, who nest during certain periods of the year, and who therefore should not be disturbed. The reefs to the north of Zabargad are also rich with charm and with birds - hawks, gannets, frigate birds, and innumerable birds of passage, subject to merciless attacks from the flocks of birds of prey on the islands.

Underwater, this is the most intact stretch of tropical sea that I have ever seen. In a number of points, towers rise from the deep to a height of a number of feet, which are a true concentrate of life forms: alcyonarians, madrepores, sponges, gorgonians with great draperies of fire coral which attain branchings and extensions at the tips that are so fine and fragile that they crumble into a thousand pieces at the slightest impact or clumsy fin-stroke. In no other point of the Red Sea have I seen such a perfectly intact environment, probably due to the total absence of visitors and fishermen.

This is also one of the very few areas where it is possible to swim with the dolphins that reside permanently in the lagoon of Dolphin Reef, not far from the Roman amphorae. These dolphins at times allow themselves to be approached in the water, the dream of every scuba diver. These reefs, practically breaking the surface, are also a handsome cemetery of shipwreck, a number of them awaiting exploration and others as yet unexplored, such as the extremely alluring wreck of a freighter that went down at Zabargad to the south of the little dock, or the wreck of a tugboat just off Cape Banas. This is a strange wreck to find in these waters, something more typical of harbor areas than of tropical seas. And yet the structure is unmistakable. From the outmoded shapes and from a number of the objects found in the hold, it would appear that this vessel sank some forty years ago. It is one of those "eloquent" wrecks, that tell in very clear terms the entire story of their drama to a careful observer. The prow in fact still rests on the reef against which the ship probably ran aground, on a day without wind or turbulence, the kind of day which is fairly rare in this part of the sea, and which are paradoxically the most dangerous, concealing as they do the treachery of the reefs just under the surface, under a deceptive blanket of calm water. The hull is simply resting on the reef, touching the seabed with its stern. All around are old lanterns hanging on the walls, a blower from the Thirties or Forties, plates, and various objects, and the usual glittering wall of glass fishes that have taken possession of the engine room.

CENTRAL RED SEA:
THE FASHINATION OF ADVENTURE

It was during the years immediately following World War II that Hans Hass, the Austrian pioneer of scuba diving, fed up with his sedentary life in Vienna, decided to set out once again on his underwater explorations of the entire world, explorations that had first taken him underwater in the seas of the tropics, where he had experienced the thrill and fear of head-on run-ins with sharks, barracudas, moray eels, giant grouper, all of which were considered at the time of his early dives (1939-1940) to be unquestionable man-eaters. Hans Hass was without a doubt one of the great underwater pioneers ever to have lived; it was he that opened the way to the sea to entire generations of divers with his stupendous books, but, what is more, he can also claim credit for having invented cases of still cameras and movie cameras that allowed the development of underwater photography, such as the very famous Rolleimarin case for the Rolleiflex cameras.

Hass set off for Port Sudan by himself, with an avalanche of baggage: hand-held harpoons, underwater cases for still cameras and movie cameras, scuba diving equipment with assorted tanks and a good supply of soda lime, films and equipment for developing film, masks, nose-plugs, fins, and other accessories... the bare essentials, such as a dinner jacket for gala evenings at the English embassy. The British commissioner at Port Sudan, Bill Clark, took a liking to him, and allowed him to live in his own home and often going down to the sea with him.

No one would have bet a nickel on Hass's chances of emerging from the shark-infested waters of Sudan alive and in one piece. And yet, despite the fact that the sea was much richer and more unspoiled than it is today, nothing happened to him at all. After the first test dives into the waters surrounding the port, he came to learn of the hulk of a large Italian ship, the Umbria, which sank at Wingate Reef, about a mile off the coast. There was an absolute prohibition of diving in or around the wreck, as there were 360,000 bombs stacked in the hull, as well as sixty cases of fuses and incendiary fragments, and other explosives, for a grand total of uncounted thousands of tons. Expert English munitions men, who had come all the way out from England for this express purpose, had drawn up a seventeen-page report in which it was calculated that, should the ship explode, the entire eastern portion of Port Sudan would be flooded.

The temptation of poking his nose into this underwater powder keg was too powerful for the Austrian to resist, and he went out to the wreck secretly, the first to dive down to the wreck with oxygen tanks; the masts still poked above the surface of the water at the time, and they were white with the guano of the seagulls.

The story of this ship and this dive is one of the most exciting I have heard. It was told to me personally by Lorenzo Muiesan, the captain of the ship, a native of Trieste, born in 1895.

The Umbria was not originally called that at all, but was christened the Bahia Blanca.

It was built in Hamburg in 1912, intended for the South American trade. It had a displacement of 10,000 tons, and it was 490 feet long. Its two engines developed a total of 4,600 horsepower, which could drive the ship through the water at a cruising speed of twelve knots. It was purchased by the Compagnia Italia, was rechristened Umbria, and was finally sold to Lloyd's Triestino in 1937. After being loaded with merchandise in the ports of Genoa, Leghorn, Naples, and Messina, it had undertaken its voyage to the Italian colonies of East Africa, encountering however considerable resistance from the English, who did everything they could do to entangle the ship in bureaucratic red tape during its passage through the Suez Canal, so that they could successfully seize her once Italy entered the war, as she seemed about to do.

As she steamed past Port Sudan, the Umbria was finally forced to come to a halt as she was hailed for a thorough check-over of her documentation. The English came aboard, led by a Lieutenant Stevens of the cruiser Leander. It was the late afternoon of 9 June 1940, and the next day Captain Muiesan just happened to pick up on his radio a broadcast from Addis Ababa which announced that Italy had just declared war, and that hostilities would commence from midnight of that day. There was no time to lose, and he ordered his attendant Danilo to burn the ship's documents and secret codes. He ordered the superintendent of the engine room, Costa, to scuttle the ship. Telling Stevens that the crew was engaged in a rescue exercise, he received permission to call all hands on deck; he then gave the intensely real order to abandon the ship, explaining to the dumbstruck English lieutenant that the ship was really going down.

An instant of irritation disturbed the well-compassed calm of the English officer, and then the two captains fell into the ceremonies of the occasion.

Neither of them wished to be the first to abandon the ship, and so Muiesan said to Stevens: "Please, by all means take your place in the life boat, consider me your prisoner," while Stevens responded, with some emotion, "No, you are my friend!" As they spoke in the little lifeboat, the Umbria settled on her left side amidst the madrepores of Wingate Reef, and was slowly transformed into an underwater garden - a few bombs less for the Italian army in Africa, perhaps, but the finest gift that could ever be offered to the scuba divers of the entire world.

When Hans Hass saw her for the first time, an experience of which he left us solid documentation in the black-and-white photographs that were published in the long out-of-print book about his expedition, the ship had not yet been completely subjected to the slow-acting processes of the sea.

For that matter, only about ten years had passed since the ship was sunk, and a good portion of her structure had not yet collapsed as it would in later years. Aside from the masts, the tall smokestack that lunged up toward the surface at an angle was still perfectly intact, while today it lies prone at the center of the hull.

98 top   The study of structural details, such as the windows and the radiator grills, has made it possible to identify these automobiles as *Fiat 1100s*; they were among the cargo of the *Umbria* when it sank.
Photograph by Andrea Ghisotti.

98 bottom   The holds of the *Umbria* contained 360,000 aerial bombs, and sixty cases of fuses and incendiary fragmentation bombs; if the cargo had exploded, it could have caused serious damage to the city of Port Sudan.
Photograph by Andrea Ghisotti.

99 top The wreck of the *Umbria* lies at a depth of about 115 or 130 feet. Locating the wreck in the sea is facilitated by the lifeboat gantries which poke out of the water. Photograph by Carl Roessler.

100-101 A lavish mantle of alcyonarians covers a wreck, transforming it into an exquisite underwater garden. Photograph by Roberto Rinaldi.

102-103 In this picture as well one can clearly see how the Red Sea appropriates foreign objects and transforms them into explosions of life and color. Photograph by Franco Banfi.

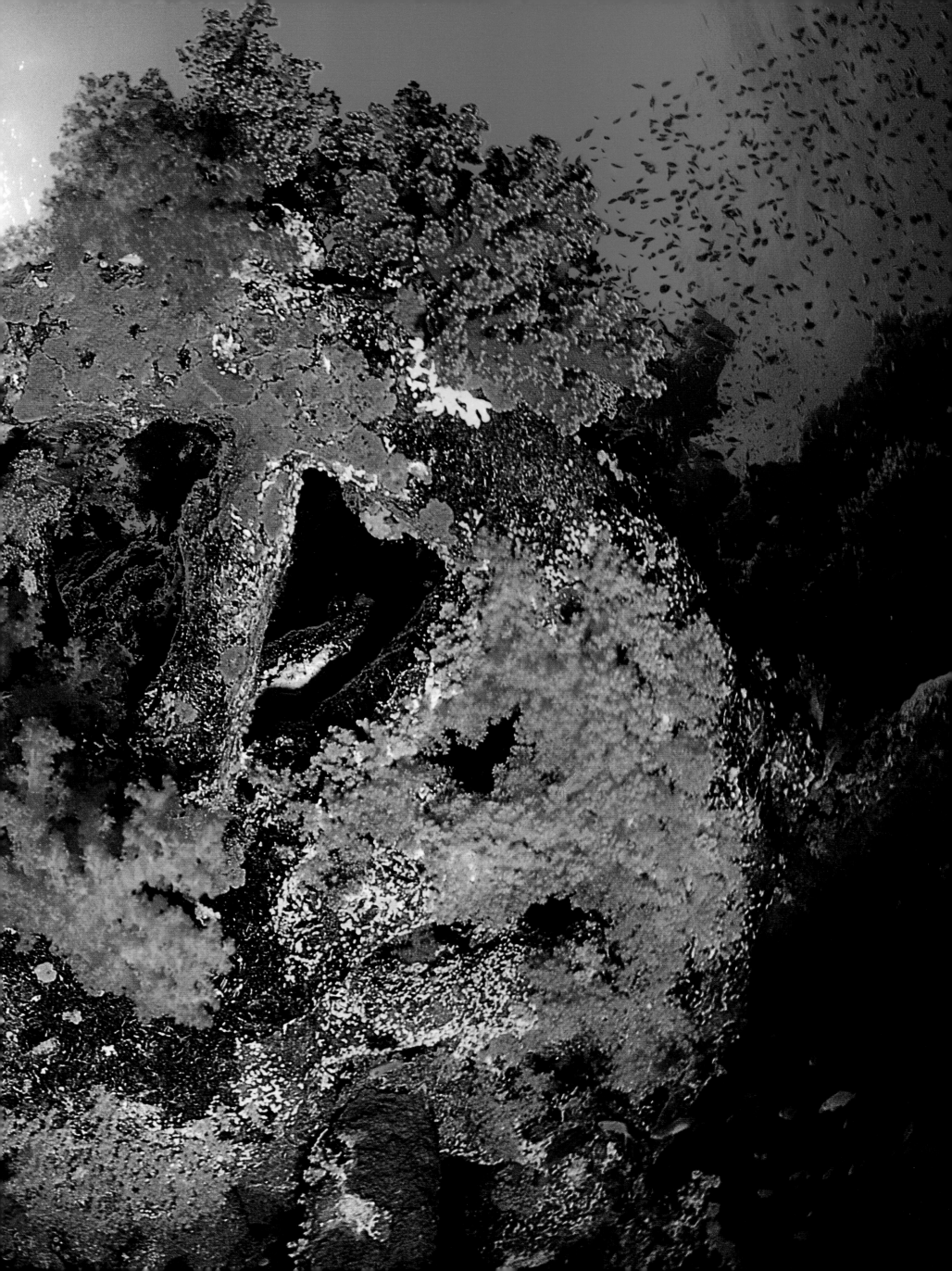

104 Lavish formations of alcyonarians cover the structure of a wreck, transfiguring it so that its original shape is almost unrecognizable.
Photograph by Franco Banfi.

105 The delicate color of the gorgonians and alcyonarians is exalted by the silvery reflections of the glassy sweeper (Parapriacanthus guentheri).
Photograph by Roberto Rinaldi.

There was also a beautiful bronze bell, inscribed with the original name of the ship, Bahia Blanca, *which was not recovered until the Seventies by Douglas Allen, while it was still fastened to one of the two masts, entirely covered by maritime concretions. Poking around in the hold of the* Umbria, *I really found just about everything imaginable, from old* Singer *sewing machines, probably on their way to Calcutta, the voyage's final destination, to old green flagons, containing essence of bergamot, bottles of wine that a few fortunate individuals had the privilege of sampling in the earliest years - and they said that the wine was excellent - to the spiral binding of the log, cases of snap fastenings and light bulbs, and much deadlier cases of fuses, from thousands of bombs stacked neatly to bags of cement, and splendid tires for*

airplanes trademarked Cordé. *The first time, so many years ago, that I dove in this wreck, I went from stern to bow with a fine-toothed comb, worming my way into every hold and hallway. Fore of the quarter-deck, there was a hold with a number of decks, but by this time, my spotlight was beginning to flicker, and the batteries were almost completely dead. I swam over to a friend, and I borrowed his little underwater flashlight, a little toy powered by four penlight batteries that cast a dim narrow beam. Swinging that inadequate shaft of light to and fro, I made my way through a series of obstructions caused by the shifting and shuttling of the cargo that broke loose as the ship sank and settled, and I finally found myself swimming along in the belly of the ship, in a dark hold where not a glimmer of sunlight penetrated. The exhaust bubbles shot up to the ceiling with every breath, breaking loose a rain of sediment that made the water increasingly murky. Suddenly the*

flashlight beam illuminated a giant eye staring straight back at me through the murky haze of falling rust particles. Once I recovered from my shock, I realized that this eye was manmade, a giant headlight from a track or a car, which I couldn't tell by the dim light of the penlight, which was beginning to flicker and fade, while the air in my oxygen tank was also beginning to get low. A year would pass before I could dive down to the Umbria *again, quite determined to solve the mystery of those eyes of steel. Though I swam the length and breadth of the ship, I just couldn't seem to find way to the hold with the headlight. I was giving up hope, and was about to quit, when I discovered an upper deck in one hold, obstructed by a great deal of material of all sorts. I squirmed into the narrow opening, and there stood three automobiles, parked one beside the other, in an extremely elegant livery, somewhere between greenish and yellow in color, created by the undersea incrustations. This time I was adequately prepared, and I was able to photograph them thoroughly, peering into the passenger compartments, where I was able to detect with considerable excitement the simple indicators and dials of the time on the dashboard, the gear shift on the steering column, the steering wheel, and the three rows of seats. Once I returned home I determined at all hazards I had to identify them, and given that the tall narrow radiators seemed typical of* Fiat *automobiles, I got into touch with the historical archives of* Fiat *motors, where Antonio Amadelli proved to be an expert and enthusiastic research colleague. Our first attempts to identify the vehicles took place over the phone, with the photographs on my light table and with a loupe in my hand, while Amadelli asked a series of precise and detailed questions over the phone. By the time our phone call was over, the hypotheses had been winnowed down to two candidates, either the 2800 or the 1100 Lunga. I sent the photographs to Turin, and after a few days I received exhaustive documentation on the cars, with a great many engineering plans and old photographs, and a certain response: they were* 1100 Lungas, *the six-seater model of the normal* Fiat 1100, *manufactured between 1939 and 1948. The tires, with an intricate tread, seemed to belong to a special version developed for use in the Italian colonies of eastern Africa.*

A little north of Wingate Reef, lies one of the most impressive reefs on the Red Sea, Sanganeb, with another lighthouse manned by Sudanese staff. From atop the lighthouse, one enjoys a spectacular view of the lagoon and the reefs that surround the island. The south side of Sanganeb features one of the most spectacular of underwater gardens, where instead of flowers there are alcyonarians. Because the cliff dropping down to the open sea is absolutely sheer and vertical, one has the impression of looking at the facade of an old apartment house with many flower boxes on each floor.

Moving to the western tip of the undersea cliff off Sanganeb, one finds a sandy platform some 65 to 80

106 top From atop
Sanganeb, facing the
Sudanese coast, one enjoys
a remarkable view of the
lagoon and the reef.
Photograph by Carl Roessler.

106 bottom The aerial view
allows one to take in at once
the entire city of Suakin,
south of Port Sudan, now
forgotten and divested of its
ancient splendor.
Photograph by Robert
Caputo/Aurora/Grazia Neri.

*feet below the surface, which alone is worth the trip to
Sudan. This is the permanent abode of a numerous
school of barracuda, while the coastal grottoes are
inhabited by hundreds of black and yellow dotted
grunts. Needlefish and large parrotfish, pufferfish and
burrfish, jacks, angelfish, surgeonfish, groupers,
butterflyfish, rays, are just a part of the many creatures
swimming continually around a scuba diver. From the
sandy bottom, like sheaves of wheat, magnificent sea
whips of a spectacular reddish color stand, while
mushroom corals surrounded by glass fish, gorgonians,
alcyonarians, and sponges are each complete
microcosms, rising here and there from the sea floor. In
the midst of all this lush abundance, grey sharks of the
Carcharhinus wheeleri variety swim tirelessly, and come
quite close to scuba divers, who are thus able to get
some excellent photographs. Moving to the outer ridge,
either toward the south or toward the west, and rising a
bit from the sea bed, where the bottom drops away
sharply, it is easy to spot formations of hammerhead
sharks, ten or fifteen of the huge beasts at a time,
swimming along in the greatest tranquillity, some of
them particularly alarming in the size of their bodies.
Quite similar, though perhaps a bit more wild, are the
sea beds of the South Point of Sha'ab Rumi. Here the
hammerheads are practically the rule, and I have even
counted groups of as many as twenty-five, a few of
which would suddenly shoot forward like lightning for
65 or 115 feet, immediately afterward resuming their
place in the formation. Unlike on the shelf of Sanganeb,
here the bottom is entirely covered with coral
concretions, and this is one of the dives that most move
me anywhere in the world, due to the continuous
procession of fish, the passing sharks, the sensation of
feeling thrust out into the depths of the Red Sea, on a
platform that is often swept by powerful currents, and
the edges of which plunge down to a depth of 2300 feet.
Slightly to the north, right on the pass that leads into
the handsome lagoon, one can see the remains of
Precontinente II, one of the first experiments in
underwater living conducted by Cousteau in 1963.
What Cousteau achieved would have already been
worthy of note on the coasts of Europe, but to have
done it in the Red Sea and in those years is an
undertaking that can be considered to belong to the
realm of the fantastic. Even now, finding a stainless steel
bolt in Port Sudan can be a fool's errand, catching an
airplane is much like buying a lottery ticket, and often
requires dozens of hours of waiting in line. Cousteau did
not take fright at the difficulties involved, and here he
built, with the support of the reliable Calypso and the
Italian cargo ship Rosaldo, a full-fledged underwater
village, with plenty of living quarters for his men, a
garage for the Soucoupe plongeante, the disk-shaped
submarine for deep-level exploration, sheds for the
equipment, aquariums for the fish, anti-shark cages,
and outposts further down. Before beginning to film the
scenes for his unforgettable documentary, The World
without Sunlight, he gave orders to graze the area
extensively, so that the concentration of fish would be*

extreme, and Nabir, the modern-day commander of the Felicidad, one of the Italian charter boats whose home port is Port Sudan, worked on this precise phase of the project. "The quantity of fish - Nabir recalls - was just incredible, walls of snappers, grunts, jacks, and sharks, a myriad of sharks." The tour of the remains of Precontinente II *has the same intriguing quality as a tour of a ghost town left over from the California gold rush. Some of the buildings have been dismantled, but the tool shed, the garage, the fish pens, and the anti-shark cages are still visible, and now form an integral part of the underwater seascape, and are unbelievably decked with concretions and colors. In the submarine garage, a huge air bubble has formed, the heritage of frequent scuba-diving visitors, and one can surface on the interior, take off one's air hose, and exchange a few words at thirty feet underwater.*

Almost every island conceals one wreck or another, most of them completely unknown. Here at Sha'ab Rumi on the eastern side of the island, I happened to discover the wreck of an old ship with a strangely shaped very sharp prow at about 200 feet under the surface, with huge terracotta amphorae in the hold, one of the many wrecks of which all documentation has long been lost. There is also the Porto Ercole, *the charter boat on which I made my first voyage here, which has slipped down to a depth of 650 feet, and to the south, at Towartit Reef, there is the mythical Russian hulk of Hans Hass, entirely covered with sea whips coral, the teak deck long gone after a century at the bottom of the sea. To the north at Sha'ab Su'adi there is the* Blue Bell, *a large modern cargo ship loaded with* Toyota *automobiles and trucks, which hit the reef, turned over, and spilled out cars, trucks, and pickups all around in grotesque positions. The hull has settled on the sea floor and there is a broad passage midway down the hull between it and the reef, where, due to the strong current that drives through, some very large alcyonarians have formed. Further down still, there is the large screw and the rudder, but here we are already 230 feet under the surface, and the bottom is still further down, at 280 or 300 feet, and it is best to venture no further.*

By night, this is certainly one of the locations where one is most likely to have run-ins with large sharks. When Massimo Clementi and Carlo Gasparri came to the Sudan to make a documentary about sharks, Nabir brought them to this precise spot, dropping some heavy baited hooks during the night. In the morning, one of the lines was drawn taut, and the scuba divers took a look - it was a huge beast, a thirteen-feet mako with impressive teeth, around which a smaller tiger shark was prowling.

There was just enough time to get organized with an anti-shark cage, and by that point there was nothing left of the mako but the huge inert carcass, an enormous mouthful ripped out of the body just around the gills, apparently by the tiger shark. Large sharks, the dangerous ones and the ones that eat humans, are around but cannot be seen at all.

And yet people disappear. It happened to an English deep-water diver just outside of the port.

A ship loaded with cattle had pitched over on one side during the loading operations and had begun to take on water. The ship was dragged out of the harbor and there is sank, its stern jutting out of the water. For many days there was a happy little sharkfest around the wreck. Then the wreck sank into deeper waters, and the Englishman decided to dive down with a colleague to recover a valuable cargo of whiskey, which was worth a fortune on the black market, but one of the divers never surfaced again.

The port is a hunting ground for the tiger shark, especially around the harbor's mouth, where the greatest depths are reached, and not far from the docks, where goods are loaded and off loaded. Hans Hass dove here in 1950 with oxygen tanks, and said that he felt a little nervous as he dove down amongst the huge boulders stacked down to the muddy bottom some thirty feet beneath.

110-111 Elegant and powerful, the grey reef shark hunts chiefly at night and feeds on fairly small fish. Photograph by Kurt Amsler.

111 top The hammerhead shark (Sphyrna lewini), distinguished by its remarkable head, which extends sideways, is found in the emptiest and least frequented waters, maintaining a depth of over 165 feet
Photograph
by Marty Snyderman.

111 center A grey shark passes menacingly near a scuba diver.
Photograph
by Pierfranco Dilenge.

111 bottom The presence of sharks always creates an atmosphere of great tension, and can generate moments of excitement.
Photograph by Andrea Ghisotti.

112 Jacks (Caranx melampygus), voracious predators and fast swimmers, often gather in great schools and cover considerable distances in search of food. Photograph by Marcello Bertinetti.

113 Barracuda (Sphyraena qenie), too, have a tendency to congregate in huge schools, generally moving about in proximity to the coral reef. Photograph by Ron and Valerie Taylor/Ardea.

Perhaps he took a greater risk in this occasion than in many other seemingly daring dives, or maybe he did not - how can one forget the little Sudanese children who leap off the pier each day, splashing happily in the water? And yet just a few years ago, one of these children disappeared into the mouth of a huge tiger shark, who surfaced to take the child in broad daylight, under the terrified eyes of everyone, while the grandfather of Nabir, right in front of the harbor entrance, was ripped apart by a tiger shark that had capsized his vessel. The cook of the Red Sea Hotel, swept out to sea by a furious rainstorm in 1949 was fished out of the water not long afterwards without his head, snapped off by a shark. Another fisherman, again in the harbor, was recovering a large chunk of meat tossed off of a ship, when a tiger shark came and snapped it out of his hands, and then attempted to overturn the boat. Flattened on the bottom of the boat, he could feel the huge fish sliding under the hull, a terrible experience which finally drove him mad. Nor do the tiger sharks only wander around at the mouth of the harbor. Gianni Mandarino, the skipper of the Wandu, told me that at the far end of the port, where the water is only a few feet deep, and where the women of the village would often come to do their washing, the carcass of a cow had washed up. A fine example of the tiger shark showed up to claim up, by no means intimidated by the shallow water, and since that time, people are extremely loath to repair hulls or take a swim in the port. For that matter, it is well known that there are tigers at the mouth of the harbor. A total of nineteen individuals have died at their jaws, and perhaps a few more have perished in the last few years since I was last in the village, and if one drops a baited line with a strong hook, during the night, one can reel in monsters that are ten or thirteen feet in length. I was thinking of all of these things as I was plunging down into the murky water just outside of the harbor, a massive one-inch cable wrapped around my arm. Despite my thinking better of it more than once, I had fallen into an ugly situation. A Polish ship had lost anchor and chain, which had rattled out through the anchor escapement, disappearing into the depths, presumably hitting bottom. A delegation had come that evening to our boat, begging us to give them a hand, because it would be a pretty serious matter for them to have to return to their homeland without their anchor. They said that they knew exactly where it had fallen in, and that they had detected it with radar. The following morning, they redoubled their persuasion, begging us to help them. In the end, I accepted, and I readied myself for the dive along with Antonio, a pupil of mine from the underwater training courses, a particularly good one who was later to become one of my finest instructors. While he was accompanying us to the location with their launch, it became clear that he had not the slightest idea of the exact position: there were those who said more to the left, others who said more to the right, some who said landward, and others who said further out to sea. In the end, we just dove into the dirty water, beginning a breathless descent down toward a sea bottom that we could never see, lost in the murky water. Finally, after an eternity, in which we felt totally helpless, like so many worms on baited hooks, awaiting the sharks of the port, we hit bottom, sinking deep into the mud - 250 feet under and not a sign of the anchor. A quick look around, with visibility down to six feet, and then we headed back for the surface, with a strong feeling of uneasiness deep inside. It all ended with a gift of a bottle of whiskey which we drank off that evening, doing all we could to chase away the ugly nightmare of that dive. Often, with sharks, it is chiefly a psychological matter. For years, we dove at night at Sha'ab Anbar, a reef that provided excellent shelter, and which we used as a base for our daily excursions toward the reefs further out to sea in the group of the Suakins. The bottom of the lagoon was fairly shallow and extremely rich in creatures and plants. A few years later, while I was preparing for a night-time dive in this place, Gianni Mandarino told me that if he were in my shoes, he wouldn't have made the dive, since a short while before he had seen a large tiger shark in that exact place, and that just outside of the further pass the reef plunged downward sharply to great depths, from which these sharks emerged at nighttime. I was all ready to dive at this point, and I did not want to miss my nighttime dive, and so I went head-down into the water, followed half-heartedly by Massimo, my boon companion in so many adventures, who spent the entire dive swinging the flashlight to the left and right like a saber, extremely tense and unhappy, while I spent my time in perfect contentment, photographing my sleeping reef fish. And he has never forgiven me after all these years for dragging him down into the terrible pass from which the tiger sharks emerge. But I was busy the whole time setting f-stops and focusing, and I never thought of sharks once. This group of the Suakin islands is perhaps the most intriguing spot in the entire Red Sea. There are a number of islets and a vast number of surface-grazing reefs, which protrude from the extreme deep like towers, generally stopping just a yard or two below the surface, posing considerable risks for navigation. The allure of these places is enormous, and for days or weeks one can remain in the middle of the Red Sea without ever seeing the coast, diving into sea beds where just about every sort of encounter has become possible. Every scuba diver who has descended into these waters has plenty of stories. There are those who say that have seen amazing numbers of sharks at Jumna, those who have seen manta rays at Logan, others who have seen sharks at Keary, and yet others who have seen thousands of jellyfish at Brisbane. In short, a sea that is teeming with life and extremely lush, where every dive has a flavor of adventure. The truth is that every location has its biological rhythms - one day it might be teeming with fish, another day it may be nearly devoid of life forms, and yet again may be the season for reproducing for one species, and then there may be something that just electrifies the entire range of fauna.

114-115 A grouper
(Plectropomus p. marisrubri)
with garish coloring patrols
its territory. This species,
very common in the Red
Sea, may prefer coral
seabeds, but it will also
frequent sandy seabeds and
the twisted structures of
wrecks.
Photograph by Andrea and
Antonella Ferrari.

The few islets of the Suakins that emerge from the surface are surrounded by bright coral beaches, where sea turtles creep out of the water by night to lay their eggs. By day, on the other hand, one can find them just off the coast, waiting for nightfall, tucked away inside grottoes, dens, and fissures, with their durable shells to protect them from the attacks of sharks. Walking around on these islands is wonderful. The vegetation is scanty and only during the winter months does the occasional heavy rainstorm fill in the landscape in the space of just a few hours with green bushes and a low vegetation creeping along the sand, a pleasant contrast with the turquoise color of the low tide. On the main highland, at times constituted by a boulder or a very low hillock, the fish hawks make their nests, crafting amazing structures out of roots, at least three feet in height and even larger in girth, dotted with the remains of sun-dried fish. On the farthest sandy spits, on the other hand, seagulls, terns, at times pelicans, gannets, and even frigate birds take shelter. The best known of all these islands is Seil' Ada Kebir, the island of the sea turtles, where years ago we made a chilling discovery - one area of the island was entirely covered with human bones, all that remained of the crew of a freighter, according to the Sudanese that accompanied us.
I believe, however, that the story went differently, because I had been hearing a different version for years, and I had also read about it in the fantastic book, **The Secrets of the Red Sea**, by Henry De Monfried, published in Italy in 1935. In order to understand the story, one must understand the growing commerce in transporting pilgrims to Mecca, which had become a very lucrative business for the shipowners of the eastern coasts of the Red Sea, and in particular for those of Suakin and the other small ports along the Sudanese coast of the Red Sea, who are the closest to Jedda, and who are therefore able to offer the shortest and cheapest maritime route. It happened that a great many of these shipowners were not exactly respectable businessmen, and they would sell and buy just about everything - weapons, drugs, slaves, and of course hapless pilgrims. The most unscrupulous ones would at times fall back upon a nightmarish trick. They would embark pilgrims, accepting extortionate payments for the trip, and then they would sail all day out into the open sea. As evening fell, they would land at one of the islets in the Suakin group, like the island of the sea turtles, Burkut or Barra Musa, telling the pilgrims that the lighthouse of Hindi Gider, the outermost of the islands, was none other than the lighthouse of Jedda, where they would be arriving the next morning. Given that it was dangerous to approach the reefs at night, they would land and make camp for the night. They would land the pilgrims and by night, as the pilgrims slept, they would steal off in the boats, leaving the hapless wretches to die of starvation on the island, and then they would return only when all the pilgrims had long since perished, and make off with their belongings. There is no reason to think that this does not still happen today, and it certainly was still happening just

a few years ago. That Suakin lives almost exclusively on smuggling is well known to one and all. Otherwise, there would be no explanation of the remarkable activity of all the shipyards that continue to build sambuks along the coast, while there are very few used in fishing. We encountered smugglers a number of times on Sha'ab Anbar or on other reefs: they sail in by night with their large boats painted garishly, nowadays equipped with powerful Japanese engines. Despite the extremely primitive appearance of these boats, they are very seaworthy, built with ancient techniques, and they are capable of making the crossing even with extremely rough seas. The cargo ranges wildly - electric appliances, sheep, weapons, drugs, illegal immigrants, and every other sort of merchandise or illicit traffic, perhaps including the slave trade. Suakin, the Venice of the Red Sea in centuries past, today is nothing more than a heap of rubble. Strategically, its location was excellent, built on an island in the midst of a "marsa," or sheltered bay, with shallow and sometimes marshy waters, a coastal lagoon that partly defended it against raiders. As early as 1510, the Portuguese Don Juan da Castro described it as "... an island where there is not a single square foot of free land, where everything is so built up that the entire island is a city and the entire city is an island..."
The buildings of Suakin have an architectural stye that could be called Red Sea style, a mix of Arab and

118-119 The transparent body
of a shrimp (Periclimenes sp.)
mingles visually with the
alcyonarian upon which it is
poised.
Photograph
by Eleonora De Sabata.

120 Alcyonarians, distinguished by the most incredible shades of color, undulate gently at the touch of the slightest current. Photograph by Marcello Bertinetti.

121 A small crinoid, or sea lily (Ophiothrix purpura) mingles inconspicuously amidst the flowering branches of an alcyonarian. Photograph by Eleonora De Sabata.

Turkish culture. The material used for building is made up of blocks of madrepore, taken out of a quarry on the southern side of the bay - a cheap material that can be easily shaped, which, if appropriately covered with a coat of whitewash, can survive the weather at considerable length, as is shown by the home of Khorshid Bey, which dates from the thirteenth or fourteenth century. Space is the principal problem of Suakin, and so the typical one-story structure of the Turkish house is raised higher, producing two- or three-story houses, with **masharabiya** *or* roshan, *distinctive little terraces, protected by silver teak grates from Java, which the wealthier merchants import specially for the purpose. Another distinctive feature of Suakin is the richness of plaster decorations, which can still be seen on a number of arches that have been partially destroyed, contrasting sharply with the Koranic rules of simplicity. But Suakin has always been a wealthy and independent city, concerned chiefly with its trade and none too interested in religious matters. As late as 1870, after the Suez Canal was opened, Suakin prospered. For centuries it had been the principal port for pilgrims embarking on their way to Mecca, as well as the leading marshalling yard for the slave trade; alongside these activities, it conducted more traditional forms of trade. Every three months from this port a giant caravan of five hundred to a thousand camels would set off, headed toward the heart of Africa, where it would sell or barter sugar, candles, soap, rice, clothing, china, pots, knives, and other products still.*

In 1904, the fate of Suakin was decreed at a conference table - the port was too small, always plagued by the coral reefs, not particularly well sheltered from the winds, but above all the city was too crowded and overbuilt to imagine that European features could be applied to it.

And so the decision was made to build Port Sudan, forty miles to the north: the work was done in a few years, and 1910 it had already been completed. The wealthy merchants of Suakin were nonetheless attached to their town and their customs, and for years they continued to oversee commerce from their old homes, until the National Bank was shut down in 1923, and the Eastern Telegraph Company was also transferred to Port Sudan. From that time on, the decline was irresistible, so that today the city is only an array of rubble heaps inhabited by cats and seagulls.

122-123 This shrimp poised upon a nudibranch "Spanish dancer" (Hexabranchus sanguineus), offers a perfect example of cryptic camouflage. Photograph by Itamar Grinberg.

124 A tiny starfish with
bright colors (Fromia sp.)
seeks refuge upon an
alcyonarian.
Photograph by Franco Banfi.

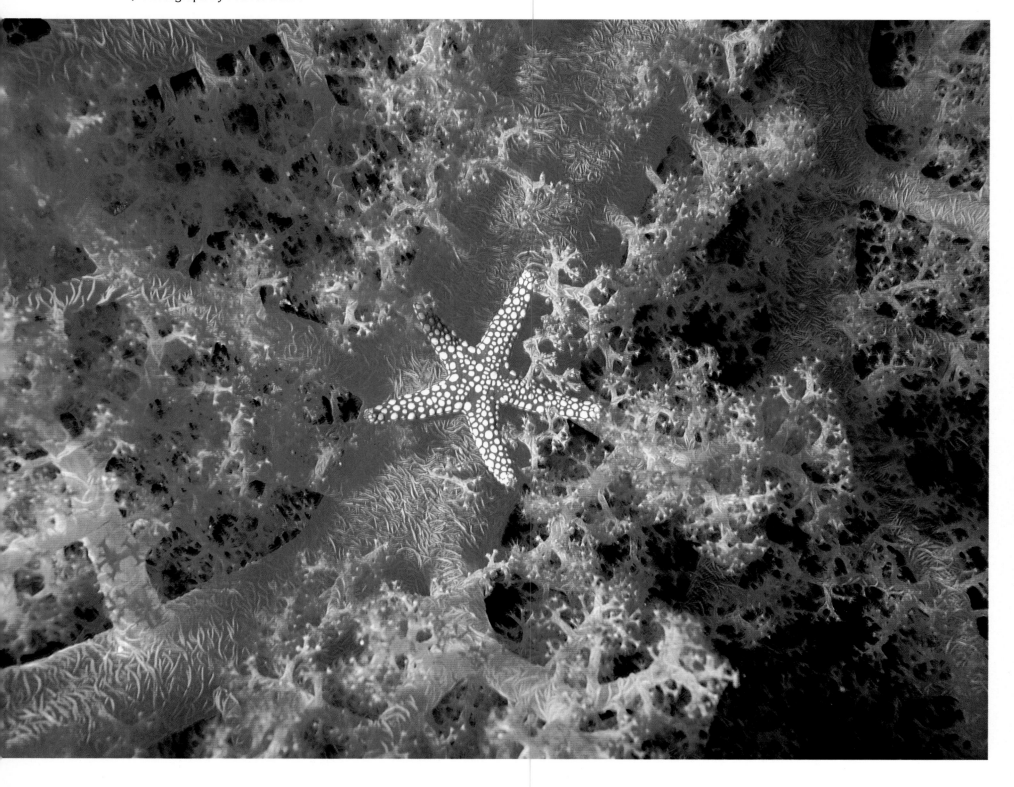

125 Again, an alcyonarian
hosts a cleaner shrimp
(Stenopus hispidus) in a
typical symbiotic
relationship.
Photograph by Franco Banfi.

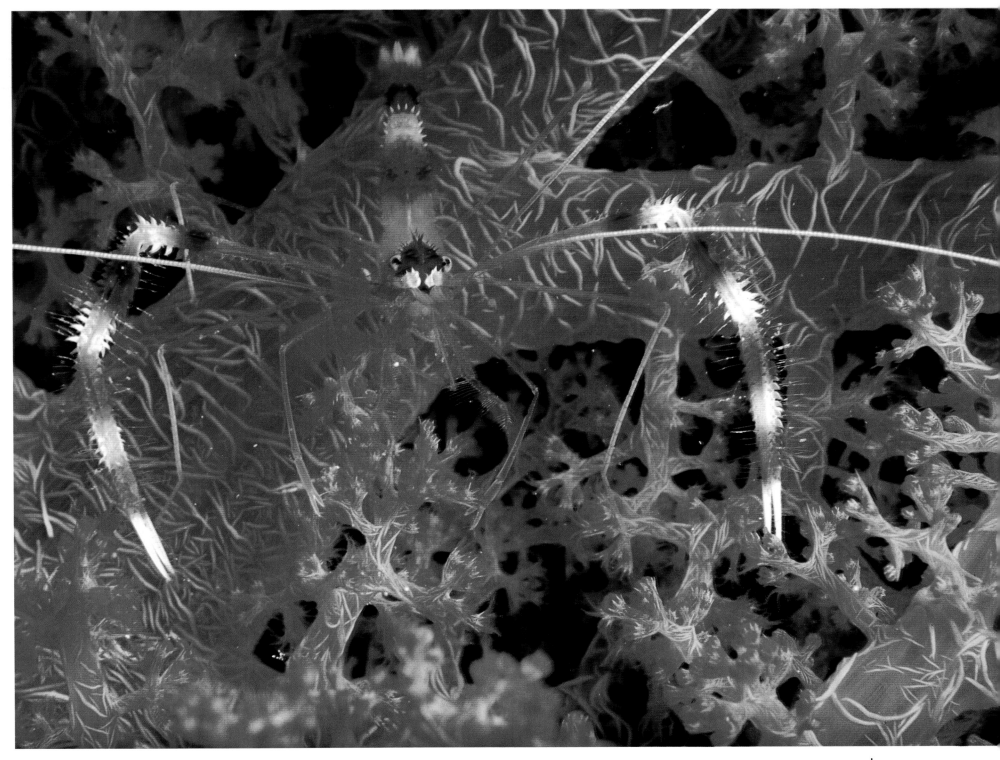

126-127 A shrimp peeps
out from the basal disk of
the sea anemone with which
it lives in a symbiotic
relationship.
Photograph by Jeff Rotman.

128-129 Two multicolored
nudibranches (Chromodoris
quadricolor) stand out
against the red background
of a sponge.
Photograph by Jeff Rotman.

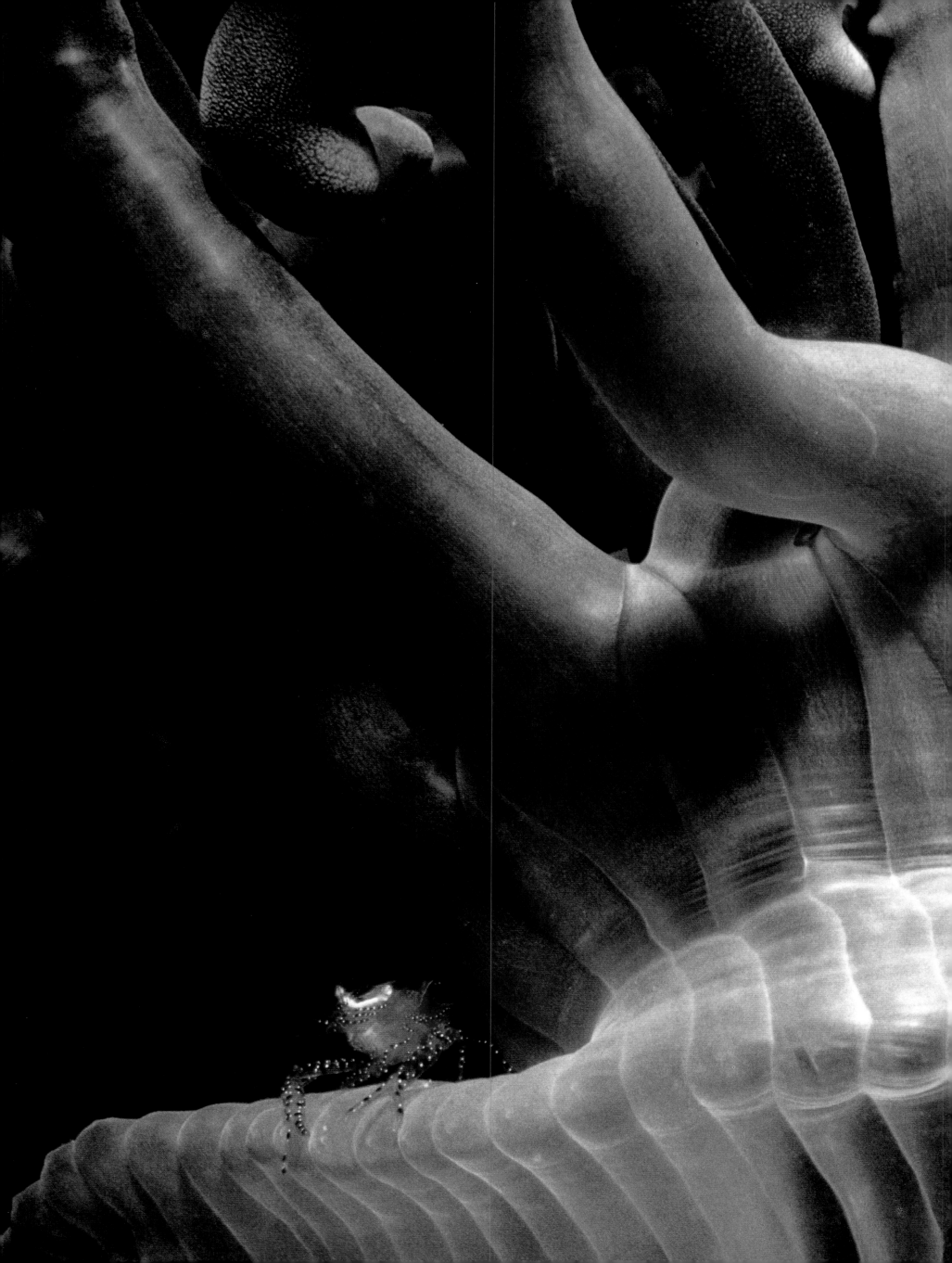

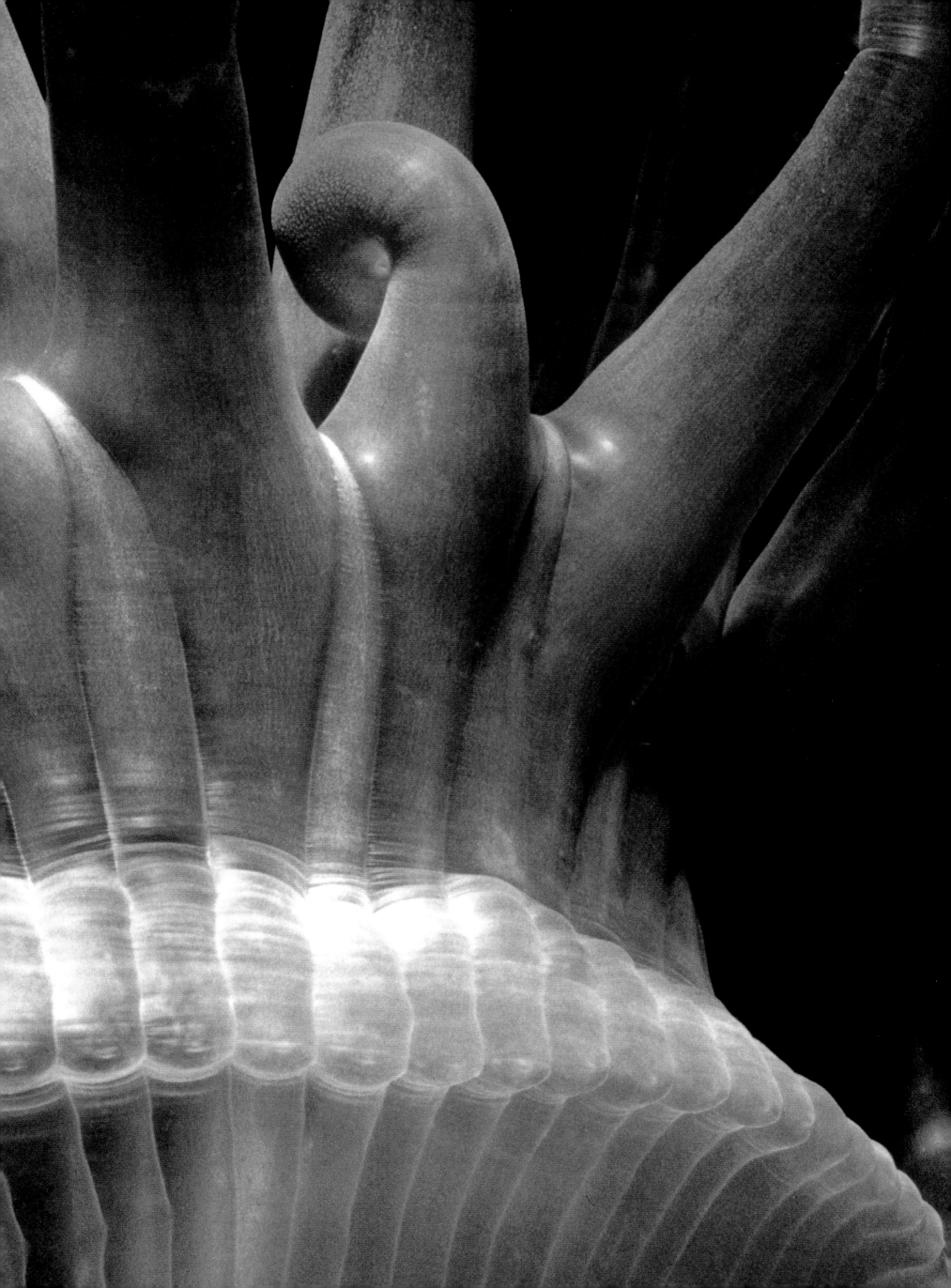

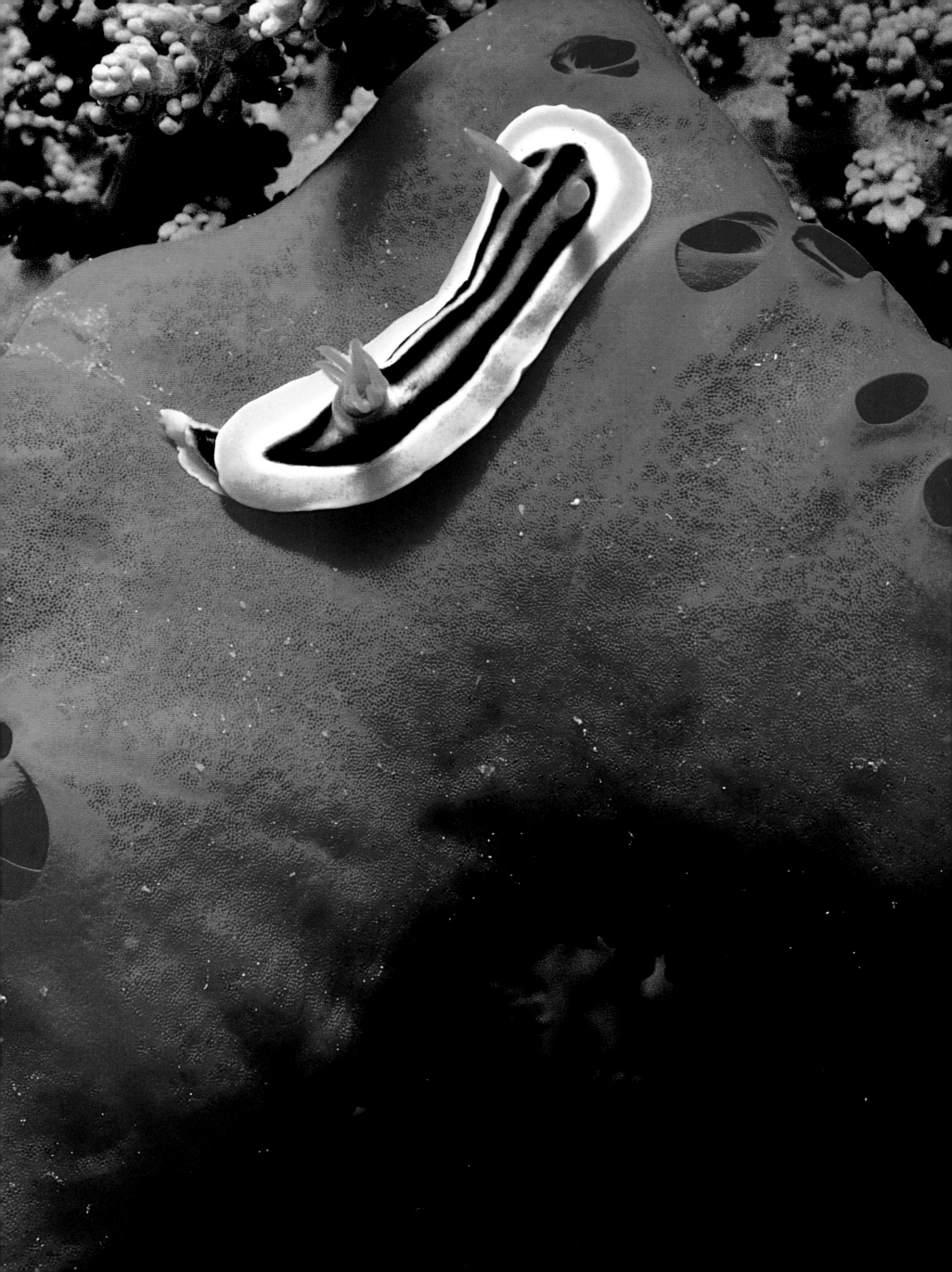

SOUTHERN RED SEA: THE LAST FRONTIER

*T*he Dahlak Islands have a special place in the heart of every Italian scuba diver, or at least in the hearts of all those who made up the first and second ranks of this country's national team. At one time, this was Italian territory, part of the colonies of AOI, of Africa Orientale Italiana *(Italian East Africa)*, as it was known during the Fascist years. When Bruno Vailati set out on the first Italian expedition of the postwar period in the Red Sea, he chose these very islands as his destination, perhaps because he still thought of them as still being a little bit Italian. The majority of the public works here, the roads, the well-known railroad that linked Massaua to Asmara, apartment buildings, homes, movie theaters, harbor facilities, automobiles - all of them were Italian, and there are still a great many Italians who continued to live here after the end of the war. Underwater, the Dahlak Islands certainly do not deserve the reputation for excellent diving that seems to hover around them, like a slightly mysterious and backward-gazing phantom. The water is not very deep, the bottom is sandy and visibility is often cut quite short, by the sand and the enormous quantity of plankton in these waters. The reefs, on the other hand, are very limited in expanse, and there are not many vertical drops, which generally are small step-downs of no more than 15 or 20 feet at a time, where the coral formations come nowhere near the luxuriant abundance of those found in Sudan, or in the magic underwater gardens of the norther Red Sea. Is this reputation unfairly gotten then? Not really. Plankton means life and the food chains that derive from such an abounding variety of plankton leads to a wealth of fishlife that is truly astounding. There is another force driving the reputation, and it is one that we can hardly ignore - it is the allure of adventure. One hundred twenty-six islands scattered in the waters off Massaua, where one can breathe all of the aroma of the true Red Sea, where in the past there pearl divers and great harvests of black coral, arms traders, slave merchants - a true frontier extending out into the heart of this vast watery back-alley, a bulwark against the coasts of Yemen and toward the south, the narrows of Bab el Mandem, with terrifying currents and storms. Vailati's expedition began in December of 1952, with the departure from Naples of the Formica, a small ship that was really not much more than a long boat, just 90 feet in length, which could not attain speeds of anything over seven knots.

130-131 The ability of the stonefish (Synaceia verrucosa) to camouflage itself is quite remarkable, and that is the cause of its extreme danger to its prey. Photograph by Urs Moeckli.

131 top The white beach of the island of Medote looks out over the sea surrounding the Dahlaks.
Photograph by Andrea Ghisotti.

131 bottom This picture clearly shows how a stonefish can conceal itself perfectly with the coral reef. Photograph
by Vincenzo Paolillo.

132-133 The archipelago fo the Dahlak Islands offers refuge to a number of species of birds: form herons and storks, to Osprey (Pandion haliaëtus) and terns, seagulls and pelicans, and takes flight along the coast of the island of Dur Gaam.
Photograph by Marcello Bertinetti

133 top A batfish (Platax teira) patrols its territory, possibly in searcho of food. This fish with a distinctive shape lives primarily on invertebrates and zooplankton.
Photograph by Marcello Bertinetti.

On board the Formica when she sailed was a crew of eleven, including scientists, photographers, filmmakers, camera operators, and athletes. Their voyage showed every indication of being a tough one from the start - winter is a terrible time to venture out into the eastern Mediterranean, famous for its storms. It took a month of hard sailing to reach Massaua, where the expedition took on its final members, all bearing names that have become legendary: Bruno Vailati, mastermind and organizer; Folco Quilici, who made a film documenting the expedition; Masino Manunza, camera operator; Giorgio Ravelli, photographer and inventor of a great deal of the camera equipment that was used; Francesco Baschieri, the expedition's scientific director; Raimondo Bucher, the director of the athletic group, assisted by his wife Enza and by Silverio Zecca; Gianni Roghi, journalist and writer; Luigi Stuart Tovini, assistant to Baschieri; Priscilla Hastings, illustrator, and Alberto Grazioli, a doctor. The adventurous experiences of the expeditions are recounted in a number of documents that are rightly considered to be part of the history of scuba diving - the documentary Sesto Continente (Sixth Continent), the book Dahlak by Gianni Roghi, and the volume Sesto Continente by Folco Quilici. Certainly today one is amazed to note the differences between the systems of research employed back then and those which are used today - every animal, no matter how rare it might have been, was slaughtered and preserved in embalming fluid formaline, fish, bird, reptile, or crustacean though it might be. The group of athletes, on their part, fished away as hard as they could, and today we shudder at the scenes of wholesale massacre of helpless mantas, rays, guitarfish, giant groupers, moray eels, and so many other types of fish, many of which not even edible, at times taken just for the pleasure of the kill. Quite simply, these were times very different from today, and any sort of environmental awareness there may have been was quite limited, and not everywhere one turns, the way it is today - this modern environmentalism had not even begun to stir. The book by Gianni Roghi in particular has left a trace in the heart of all of us, describing as it does places, sensations, and adventures with a free-wheeling and enjoyable style, which reaches points of great journalism in certain pages, like those unforgettable ones describing the dances of the manta rays. Roghi was with Baschieri on the small wooden launch, when suddenly a vast manta ray leapt out of the water directly in front of the bow, splashing back into the water with a resounding flop. This was the overture to an endless succession of leaps and splashing crashes with dozens of mantas, all of them females, hurtling out of the water around the little boat. Roghi realized that from the genital apertures of a few of them, there protruded the tiny tail of a newborn manta - perhaps the mothers-to-be were leaping in order to help the birth-giving process. When peace finally returned, this hypothesis received further support as the two astonished observers saw a long line of baby mantas swimming rapidly out towards open waters, a spectacle which no researcher had ever witnessed before.

134-135 White fin sharks (Triaenodon obesus) are among the most assiduous "clients" of the coral reefs of the Red Sea.
Photograph by Marty Snyderman.

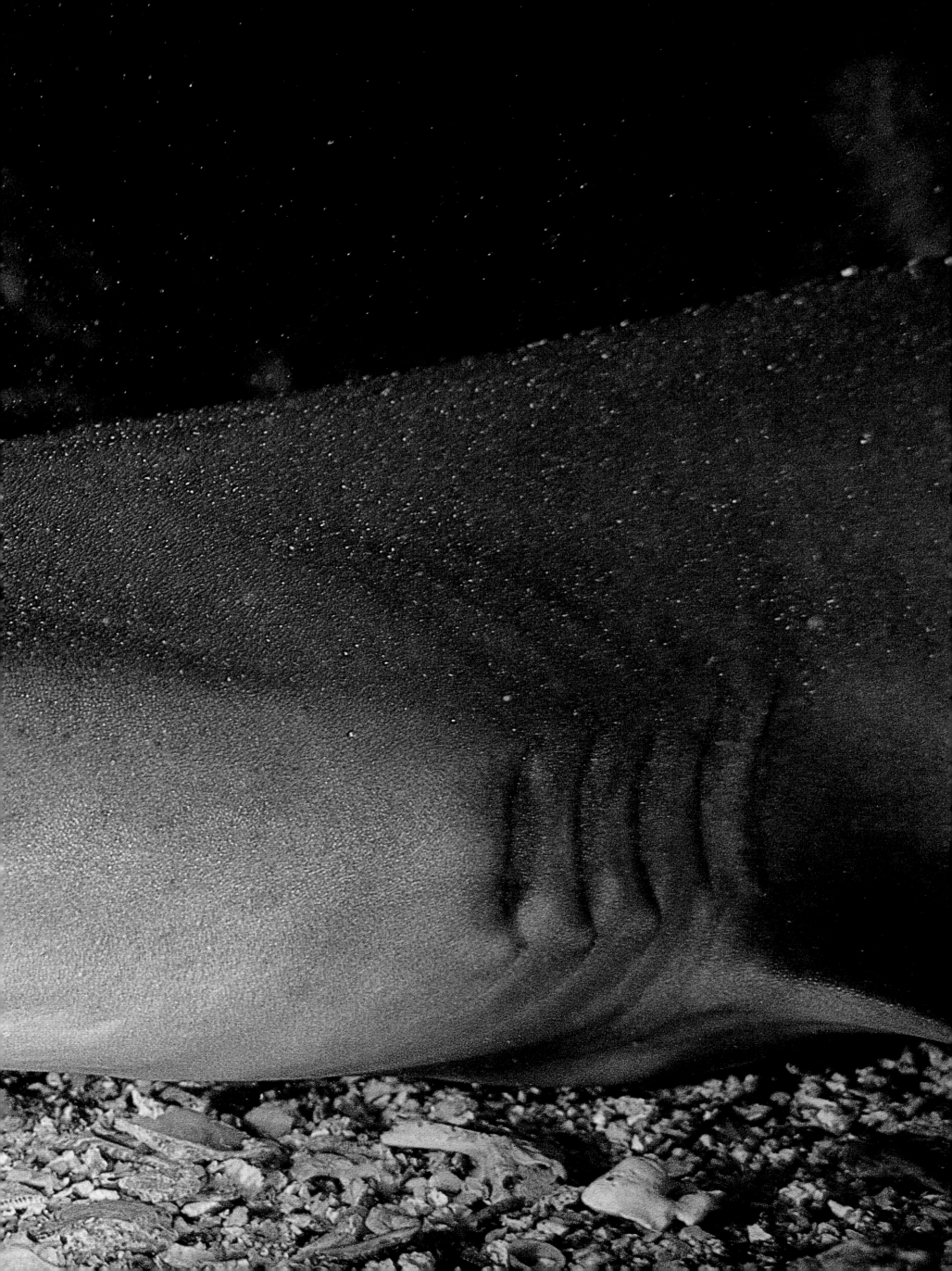

This is the Dahlak Islands, a stretch of sea where anything can happen, and one can happen upon even the most unusual natural spectacles. Before reaching the archipelago, there had been another thrilling and sobering adventure. In the open sea, there had suddenly emerged a great wave of foam, and the two were thinking that they were sailing toward an uncharted reef, when suddenly a great swordfish leapt out of the water, followed closely by a shark. There was more foam, this time reddened by blood. The vision was blood-curdling, a battle between titans, between the fastest fish in the sea and one of the most fearsome of predators, a huge mako thirteen feet in length, which had reduced the fish to a moribund state with snap after vicious snap. Not even slightly intimidated by the presence of the Formica, the shark drew near to the surface of the sea, and gave a last huge lunging bite to its prey, before being run through by a harpoon launched from on board the launch. There was a moment's pause, and then the shark realized angrily what had happened, which snapped off the huge grip of the harpoon as if it had been a breadstick, and then dove, perhaps to die on some concealed seabed.
For me, the Dahlak Islands were truly my first tropical love, since I dove here for the first time in the Red Sea in 1973. At the time, it was one of the first easy-to-reach diving site, offered as a destination by a number of Italian tour operators. I set out on a whim, there had been an extra place on board the Assab, an old boat with three engines, an incredibly broken down craft - only one of the engines was working, and the boat chugged along at four and a half knots.
It seemed to me that I was on one of those old Mississippi steamboats, but it was as pleasant as could be on board, aside from the throttling heat, and we indulged in huge contests of fishing prowess, took photographs by the roll, clambered onto islands flocked with birds to explore, and had great drinking sessions fueled by Melotti beer. Then came 1975, the coup d'état, the wholesale flight of resident Italians, growing tensions in the country, which finally erupted into civil war, and in the conquest of the country by the Eritreans. Riccardo Melotti, at the time, was brewing the beer of the same name in a factory in Asmara, which was a business that his father had set up during the years of the war, and which his mother had carried forward after the death of the father. When the beer factory was nationalized, Riccardo came to Italy, and it was there that we met, beginning a long and warm friendship. Riccardo still owns a handsome villa in Massaua, the Villa Cyprea, the most spectacular mansion in all of Eritrea, where every Italian politician and diploma visiting the country was welcomed and plied with hospitality.
This was to become the base for our first Italian expedition to the Dahlak Islands, after the end of the war. The project had been in the air for some time, until 1992, when it seemed to us that the right time had come. We wanted to see what condition the islands were in after years of the forced absence of all tourism, as well as seeing once again the places where Riccardo had spent so many years of his life, and where I had been weaned as a tropical diver. Thus began a lengthy period of preparation, with the purchase of an Asso rubber dinghy, 21 feet in length, with a 130 HP engine, huge built-in gas tanks, for a total of 88 gallons of fuels, other tanks for the drinking water, with complete equipment for nautical camping, a compressor for the air tanks a generator, underwater equipment, and a thousand other accessories, with which it would be possible to live far from all forms of civilization even for extended periods in relative comfort. After closing everything up in an enormous wooden crate and loading it onto a freighter, we caught a plane and flew off to Asmara.
Seeing the city some twenty years later was enough to make my heart stop - clean boulevards decked with flowers everywhere, clean dry air, old Italian buildings, white and blue Fiat 1100 taxis, just like in the old days. Massaua, on the other hand, is in ruins.
And indeed the war raged furiously in the last few years: we found corpses still in the fields, scorched tanks, abandoned armored vehicles, bullets, jackets, Kalashnikovs underwater, along with uniforms, rucksacks, and munitions packs. With some difficulty, and primarily through the friends of Riccardo who live in Eritrea, and through his popularity, we managed at any rate to get organized, to find the fuel that we needed, the food, and the water. In the meanwhile, our wooden crate had arrived, and in just a few days, we had the rubber dinghy inflated, equipped, and ready to go. Finally we set off, with the north as our destination, toward the unforgettable Difnein, the northernmost of the islands, where underwater scuba divers on the hunt in the old days had always been on the hunt for big game. What a delight it is to sail through the Red Sea in a big rubber dinghy!
It was much better than chugging along at the four knots of the old Assab, and now the water was sliding away beneath the keel at a cruising velocity of 23 knots, and in less than three hours we had reached Difnein, welcomed by a school of bottlenose dolphins that had come to play around our bow.
Our first contact with the sea bottom was much finer than anything I remembered: the water was fairly clear, the small underwater cliff was crowded with fish such as the barracuda, batfish, butterflyfish, Pomacanthidae, including the endemic Pomacanthus asfur, with its handsome black and blue colorings, marked with a single vertical yellow stripe, groupers, jacks, burrfish, and pufferfish, a few sharks, and all of the small marine life of the reef.
The island itself, unfortunately, cannot be approached, as it has been mined, and it seems that one fisherman lost a foot. After a day or so we prepared for our great leap northward. There are shallows marked on the nautical charts, lying a few dozen miles to the northeast, in the open sea, and which because of the distances involved are practically virgin, since nobody goes there to fish, and certainly not to dive.

142-143 Sea turtles (Eretmochelys imbricata) are very common in the waters of the Red Sea; from the beginning of March until the end of July, they crawl up onto the beaches of the archipelago of Suakin and the Dahlak islands to lay their eggs, ready to face an effort so monumental that at times it kills them.
Photograph
by Carlo De Fabianis.

143 top A sea turtle struggles to leave the beach where she has laid her eggs in the early morning hours.
Photograph by Andrea Ghisotti.

143 bottom The seabeds off the Dahlak Islands, near the Eritrean coast, are predominantly sandy, and are dotted with coral agglomerations which never attain a very great size.
Photograph
by Marcello Bertinetti.

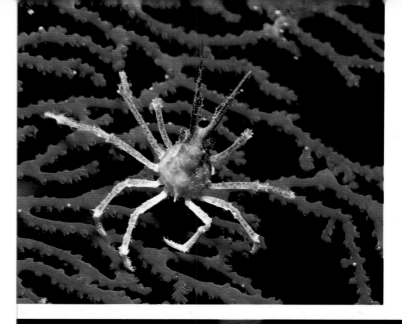

144 top A spider crab (Hyastenus sp.) moves along the branches of a coral. Photograph by Herbert Frei /IKAN.

A sambuk brought us the barrels of fuel we needed to cover the hundred miles that lay before us, and at dawn we set out. After a couple of hours of sailing on a completely calm sea, we figured we were in the area, we sharpened our gaze, we were surrounded by the usual festive dolphins, cheerful and noisy, and finally we came upon the shallow we had been heading for - it reared up like a mushroom, dropping away down to seabeds hundred of feet beneath. What excitement! We stopped for a sandwich over the top of shallow, which lies just thirteen feet beneath the surface. We tossed a chunk of cheese into the water, and we saw a snapper that easily weighed six or eight pounds literally hurtle out of the water. This seemed all right for openers! We were excited at being perhaps the first to dive in such a great area, we were in the middle of the Red Sea, we were completely out of touch with everything and everyone, the sambuk was completely devoid of the instrumentation that was needed to get here, and every slightest problem could turn rapidly into disaster. We dove and plunged downward through a spinning aquarium: snappers weighing six, eight and ten pounds were swimming everywhere, dozens of grunts, hundreds of snappers, all looked at us with that staring curiosity detectable in fish that have never seen a scuba diver before. We moved off toward the edge of the shallow, where the underwater cliff began, dropping away into gorgeous water, clear and blue, quite similar to the shallows of Sudan. Then some handsome jacks came along, followed closely by a shark, a Carcharhinus albimarginatus, *and then a second shark, a third, a fourth, and so on, until we were completely surrounded. One of the sharks was particularly large, and was trailed by a huge group of pilot fish. This one swam aggressively - we were trespassing on his territory. I moved away from the wall to take his picture, but he shied away. Riccardo told me later that when I turned away, he made for me, turning away only when he reached a distance of one and a half feet. We went on, and the sharks left us in peace. About thirty meters down, there was an explosion of red sea whips corals, almost hidden behind a wall of blue fusiliers, and then sharks, jacks, tuna, and an infinite variety of enormous snappers. Before our second dive, while we were plumbing in search of the best spots, we were again approached by bottlenose dolphins, and this time we dove into the water with diving masks and cameras, allowing ourselves to be pulled by the dinghy. The dolphins swam ahead of us, and we spent an unforgettable hour, with a platoon of twenty-four cetaceans, which we could watch perfectly as they went through their fluid evolutions with great elegance, the larger males splitting off from the school every so often to come toward us and watching, tilting their heads first in one direction and then in another. When I saw a shark swim beneath me, it dawned on me that without really paying attention, we had wandered fairly far afield of the shallow, and that we were now in the open Red Sea, with the sea floor some 600 or 1000 feet beneath us, being dangled as trawling bait behind a motorized rubber dinghy, and I suddenly felt slightly ill at ease.*

144-145 This picture shows the complex structure of an *Acropora* corals.
Photograph by Andrea Ghisotti.

145 top As night falls, the crinoids too emerge in search of food.
Photograph by Urs Moeckli.

146-147 The valves of a tridacna (Tridacna maxima) give life to an elegant pattern of sinuous shapes.
Photograph by Jeff Rotman.

148-149 This singular formation of brain coral seems to emanate phosphorescent glimmers.
Photograph by Peter Scoones/Planet Earth.

150 top A number of manta rays (Manta birostris) swim on the sea bottom in search of food. The two head fins on either side of the mouth serve the purpose of conveying the greatest possible quality of water and plankton into the creature's mouth.
Photograph
by Gerard Soury/Jacana.

150 bottom Nine manta rays, arrayed in formation, travel just under the surface.
Photograph
by Pierfranco Dilenge.

150-151 An adult manta ray can have a wingspan of 23 feet and can attain a weight of almost two tons.
Photograph by Mark Nissen.

The Dahlak Islands are a true ornithological paradise. In every island, even in the smallest ones, there are one or two pairs of fish hawks, or ospreys, which often make their nests on the cross members of the lighthouses, or else they build their voluminous nests upon the highest elevations. Frequent encounters can be had with the white pelicans, gannets, herons, seagulls, and various birds of prey. There are a great number of terms, while far rarer, but not entirely rare, are the bustards and spoonbills which nest on the islet of Seil, near Dissei, where Gianni Roghi, too, had observed them, during the expedition of 1953. Dissei is one of the islands closest to Massaua, and it is different from all the others, since it is not of coral origin. It is, therefore, fairly mountainous and harsh, with a small fishing village, a few shacks made out of recycled material of all sorts - branches, jute sacks, sheet metal. We toured it during the latter half of our expedition, after returning to Massaua, to load up on supplies and fuel, and setting out once again for the eastern part of the archipelago. The further away from the coast we moved, and the more the islands began to take on the savage charm of the wild. Mojeidi, the easternmost island, welcomed us with an emissary, a manta ray that zipped under the dinghy as we drew close to the shore, in just six feet of water.
The island's beach is one of the finest around, and is almost half a mile in length, arranged in a semicircular configuration, with plenty of "tank-treads" left by the sea turtles who crawl onto the beaches by night to deposit their eggs.
The wet sand is covered with thousands of dead shells, and is dotted with the holes of the hermit-crabs, which emerge at nightfall, dotting the beach with the infinite number of traces left by their claws or by the weight of the shell that they bear with them.
We stayed several days in Mojeidi, enjoying the uncontaminated nature, and meeting up with sea turtles crawling across the beach and then away into the water, exhausted by the effort involved in laying eggs. Just a few feet away from the dinghy, in just over three feet of water, two sea eagles made love for hours, allowing the tips of their fins to emerge from the water, but zipping away as soon as we tried to swim over to them. Then there was the nursery, an area of madrepores in shallow water, where we were able to observe the entire range of Red Sea fish at a very youthful age, perfect miniatures, just a few inches long, which we normally saw along the outer underwater cliffs. Here too every so often sambuks loaded with pilgrims on their way to Yemen would pass, boats loaded down with people willing to suffer sea sickness, thirst, and hunger for days at a time, piloted by unscrupulous ferrymen who would set out in any weather, from time to time sacrificing the boat and the human cargo to the sea gods, along routes that have been plied for thousands of years across this magic body of water, the sea that we now felt was ours, after cutting its surface in a dinghy for more than five hundred miles.

152 A school of surgeonfish (Naso hexacanthus) illuminates the nocturnal darkness as it passes. Photograph by Itamar Grinberg.

153 In the areas less heavily visited by tourists, it is not uncommon to encounter full-fledged walls of snappers (Lutjanus bohar) of considerable size. Photograph by Roberto Rinaldi.

154-155 Large jacks (Caranx sexfasciatus) ply the underwater trails of the Red Sea, scattering light and reflections. Photograph by Marcello Bertinetti.

156-157 The streamlined shape of a cornetfish (Fistularia commersonii) breaks the unrelieved blue of the water. Photograph by Christoph Gerigk.

158-159 An encounter with some manta rays (Manta birostris) is one of the most exciting moments of the dive. Photograph by Mark Nissen.

160 A twobar anemonefish (Amphitrion bicinctus) zips through the tentacles of a sea anemone. Photograph by Jones-Shimlock/Secret Sea.

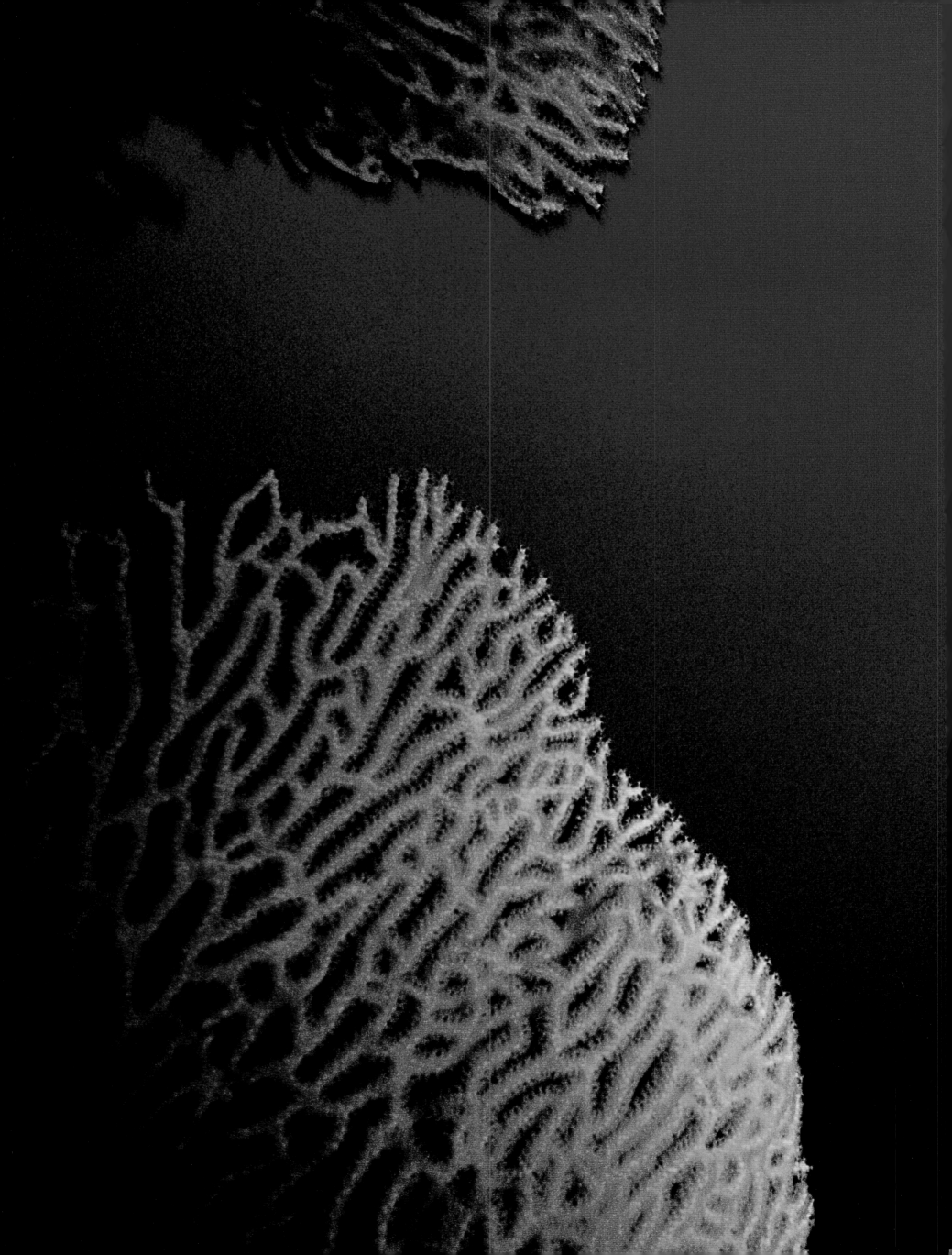

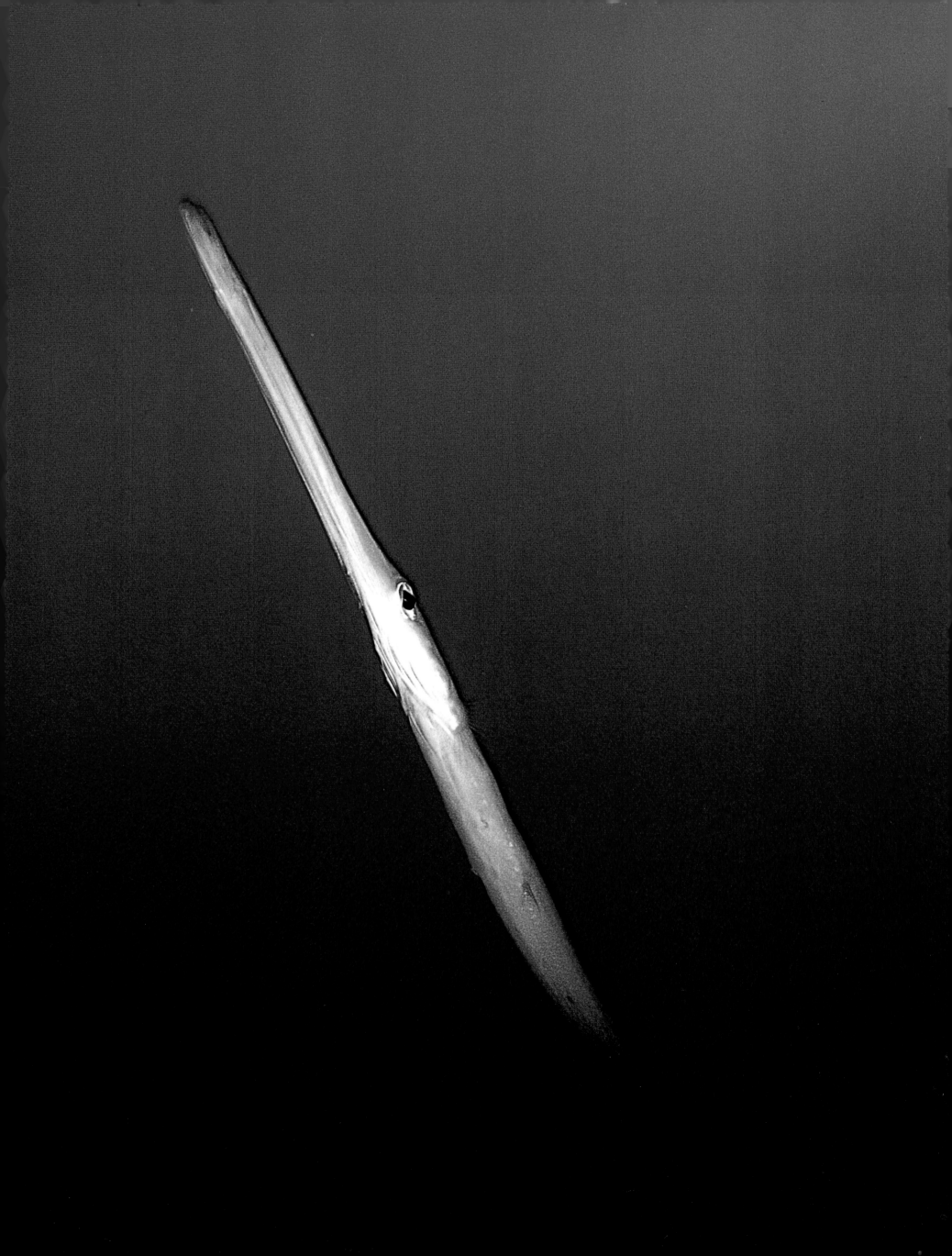